Ministerium of Pennsylvania

A Liturgy for the Use of the Evangelical Lutheran Church

Ministerium of Pennsylvania

A Liturgy for the Use of the Evangelical Lutheran Church

ISBN/EAN: 9783337046958

Printed in Europe, USA, Canada, Australia, Japan

Cover: Foto ©Lupo / pixelio.de

More available books at **www.hansebooks.com**

A

LITURGY

FOR

THE USE OF THE

EVANGELICAL LUTHERAN CHURCH.

BY AUTHORITY OF

THE MINISTERIUM OF PENNSYLVANIA

AND

ADJACENT STATES.

PHILADELPHIA:
LINDSAY & BLAKISTON.
1860.

Entered according to the Act of Congress, in the year 1860, by

LINDSAY & BLAKISTON,

in trust for the German Evangelical Lutheran Ministerium of Pennsylvania and adjacent States, in the Clerk's Office of the Eastern District of the State of Pennsylvania.

PRINTED BY HENRY B. ASHMEAD.

PREFACE.

The Synod of Pennsylvania, the oldest, and for a long time the only Synod of the Lutheran Church in this country, in the first year of its existence, "found it necessary to prepare a Liturgy, in order to secure uniformity in the ceremonies of public worship." This first brief Liturgy was republished with alterations and additions in 1786. The next edition in 1818 differs but slightly in the order of public worship from the preceding. In 1842 a new edition, carefully revised and much enlarged, was published by the Synod of Pennsylvania in connection with the Synods of New York and Ohio. In 1855 a new edition was published, the fifth since 1748, in which many and important alterations and additions were introduced, chiefly for the purpose of securing a fuller conformity to the ancient usage of the Lutheran Church. This is now the standard edition appointed for the use of the Congregations connected with the Synod.

Of this edition the present work is a translation, made by authority of the Synod for the use of those Congregations in which the English language is used. Much of the matter contained in the German Liturgy the translators have been instructed to omit as superfluous. In that portion of the work of which a translation is here presented, the translators have been instructed to make a number of alterations, chiefly for the purpose of securing a stricter conformity to the general usage of the ancient and purest Liturgies of the Lutheran Church, but in a few instances for the purpose of conforming to the practice of our English Churches in this country. A few of these alterations may be mentioned here.

The German Liturgy contains no collection of Introits, unless the Versicles which precede the Collects are of this nature, though they seldom correspond with the ancient Introits. A selection of Introits is here given, taken chiefly from the Liturgy of the Lutheran Church of Bavaria. They are intended to be sung by the Congregation, and to supplant the introductory anthem so frequently sung by the choir, and thus to furnish an appropriate opening of the service.

The Confession of Sins contained in the New York Hymn Book, which has found more general acceptance in our English Churches than any other, has been added.

The Nicene Creed has also been added for occasional use.

The most noticeable alteration is in the position of the General

Prayer. The almost invariable usage of the ancient Liturgies of the Lutheran Church is to place it after the Sermon. To this usage all the editions of the German Liturgy of the Pennsylvania Synod conform, except that of 1842. There can scarcely be a doubt that this is its most appropriate place, and that it disturbs the natural order of the several parts of the service to place it before the Sermon. It has been placed there solely because of the almost universal usage of our English Churches. Wherever practicable, it would be much better to place it, where by the common consent of almost all Lutheran Liturgies it belongs, after the Sermon.

To the General Collects a number of Special Collects have been added, any of which may be used, at the discretion of the Minister, in the public or private ministrations of his office.

For the performance of ministerial acts but one form has been given. Where several are found in the German Liturgy, the oldest and most generally received has been selected.

The work here presented for the use of the English Churches within the Synod of Pennsylvania, and any others which may see fit to adopt it, will be found to agree more nearly with the ancient usage of the Lutheran Church, than any which has yet been published in the English language by any portion of our Church in this country. Notwithstanding various minor differences between the older Liturgies of the Lutheran Church in the several countries of Europe, there is a substantial agreement in the prominent outlines of the Divine Service. And the Order of Divine Service contained in this work agrees with them in all things essential, except in position of the general prayer.

Let us examine the several parts of the Order of Morning Service in their connection, and learn that their arrangement is not arbitrary, but is in harmony with the deepest feelings of the spiritual life, and like those feelings gathers round the two great centres of the Word and the Sacrament. Löhe, in the preface to his Liturgy, furnishes a sketch, which with some alterations is here followed.

A week has been added to the past, another lies before you, between them comes Sunday, the day of communion. You come with the Congregation into the presence of the Lord to worship before him. Your purposes and desires are expressed in the words of the *Introit*. Pastor and people recount their longings in the words of the Psalms hallowed by the use of ages.

Having thus given utterance to your desire to worship before the Lord, what do you do? You wash from your feet the dust gathered along the daily journey of life. Your first act of devotion, after the Introit, is the *Confession of sins*, which can have no more beautiful form than that responsive one in which Pastor and people mutually comfort each other.

The Minister, commissioned by God, exhorts the Congregation to confess their sins, and then speaking in their name, lays before God their acknowledgment of guilt, their penitence, and their longings for forgiveness. And now the whole Congregation, bowed down under a sense of their guilt before God, and the whole burden of sin, with its bitter fruits in this life and in the world to come, and longing for forgiveness, joins in to implore the mercy of God in the *Kyrie*. The Minister declares to the penitent, longing people, the assurance of mercy in the words of *Absolution*.

In the Confession and Kyrie, the Congregation have presented themselves before God as humble suppliants, needing his grace and help. The Lord draws nigh to his waiting people, who filled with gladness at the assurance of forgiveness, burst out into the angelic hymn of praise. As of old in the manger, so now the Lord comes to those who sing the *Gloria in excelsis*. The thanksgiving of the angels still resounds when the Lord comes to the place where he has recorded his name. He comes. He is received and praised as the Triune God, to whom we draw nigh through Christ. No other hymn of thanksgiving to the Lord who comes down to receive the praises of his people, which men have ever uttered, surpasses in solemn majesty this prayer.

His countenance shines graciously, but he is still silent, he listens to the words of the Congregation. Therefore once more summing up all their necessities and all their desires, they give utterance to them in a single sentence in the *Collect*. The peculiar thought of the Festival or Sunday pervades the general wants of the soul more fully in the Collect than in the Introit. In one clear thought the soul expresses its wants, and then casts itself, waiting and longing, before him to whom all flesh must come, because he is the hearer of prayer.

The Congregation is silent. He breaks the silence, speaking to the Congregation through his gracious word. His spirit bears witness through the mouth of the Apostles, in the words of the *Epistle*. The Congregation meet him with a fervent entreaty that he would sanctify them through his word.

He speaks again. He draws still nearer to his worshipping people. They receive his own words in the *Gospel*. The Congregation answers with a joyful ascription of praise. Their hearts are filled by the power of the gospel with living faith. After their worship comes a blessed union and communion with the Lord in the *Creed*. No longer grief for sin, no longer dread of the divine wrath, no longer sighs of longing, but a joyful confidence fill the soul. They sit down in his presence, and in the *Sermon* is begun the sweet converse, the communion of saints, who rejoice together in the Lord, and ponder on his word.

The highest point in the Service has now been reached, unless the Sacrament is administered.

The Church feels herself, as the bride of the Lord, rich in him and through him, but rich also through others. In her own abundance, she remembers all the wants and misery of earth. Wishing every good to all men, she comes to the Altar with her supplications, prayers and intercessions. Seeking blessing for all, she comes reverently to the throne of richest blessing. Her heart becomes filled with the grand thought that the Church here and in heaven is but one, that pilgrims here are united in their prayers with all the redeemed in heaven, and that the prayers of both unite to cause the day of everlasting glory speedily to come.

If the Sacrament of the Lord's Supper is not administered the Service now hastens to a close. But if the Service is made complete by the administration of the Sacrament, the Congregation passes from intercession to thanksgiving in the *Prefation*. The thanksgiving loses itself in the *Sanctus*, the Thrice-holy. The Congregation filled with rapture by the Sanctus feels that the Lord comes to the Sacrament and greets him with the glad *Hosanna*.

They make ready their hearts to receive him in the *Exhortation*. Bread and wine are solemnly consecrated, the hallowed prayer of our Lord and the holy words of institution are said. The Lamb of God is present. The Congregation filled with the remembrance of the Redeemer's triumph through suffering, prays in lowliest loftiest strains, commend themselves in all their bodily and spiritual need to the gracious help of the Lord of our Lord in the *Agnus Dei*.

It is well with the people of God, holy longings fill their souls, and now they receive the Sacrament. Through faith unto faith they have come, and now have most blessed experience. They are at the table of the Lord. They can rise no higher in this life. There is nothing beyond but heaven. Their longings find fit expression in the *Nunc Dimittis*.

With thanksgiving to God the service closes.

This edition of the Liturgy has been printed to meet the wants of the Churches connected with the Synod of Pennsylvania. It is to be presented to the General Synod at its next session, in order that if that body should see fit, it may be adopted for general use. It has not as yet been stereotyped, so that any alterations deemed necessary may be made in another edition.

THE COMMITTEE.

TABLE OF CONTENTS.

PART FIRST.

THE ORDER OF DIVINE SERVICE FOR SUNDAYS AND FESTIVALS.

	PAGE
I. The Order of Morning Service,	15
The Holy Communion,	27
II. The Order of Evening Service,	33
III. The Festival Introits,	34
IV. The Collects for the Sundays and Festivals of the Church-Year	39
General Collects before the Scripture Lessons,	70
Collects for the Close of the Service,	71
Special Collects,	73
V. General Prayers for Morning and Evening Service,	81
VI. Festival Prayers for Morning and Evening Service,	87
VII. The Passion Services,	110
VIII. The Epistles and Gospels for the Sundays and Festivals of the Church-Year,	142
IX. The Scripture Lessons,	145

PART SECOND.

THE ORDER OF MINISTERIAL ACTS.

I. The Order of Holy Baptism,	157
The Baptism of Infants,	157
The Baptism of Adults,	160
II. The Order of Confirmation,	165
III. The Order of Confession and Absolution,	171
IV. The Order of Marriage,	174
V. The Order for the Communion of the Sick,	177

CONTENTS.

	PAGE
VI. The Order for the Burial of the Dead,	181
VII. The Order for the Installation of the Church-Council,	185
VIII. The Order for the Opening and Closing of the Synod,	189
IX. The Order of Ordination to the Office of the Ministry,	195
X. The Order for the Installation of a Minister,	202
XI. The Order for the Laying of the Corner-Stone of a Church,	208
XII. The Order for the Consecration of a Church,	214

Festivals of the Church.

I.
Immoveable Festivals.

Christmas, or the Nativity of our Lord, . . . December 25.
Circumcision of Christ and New Year's Day, . . January 1.
Epiphany, or the Manifestation of Christ to the Gentiles, January 6.
The Festival of the Reformation, ... October 31.

II.
Moveable Festivals.

A.

The Moveable *Festivals* all depend upon *Easter* except *Advent*.

Easter is always the *First Sunday* after the Full Moon, which happens upon, or next after the twenty-first day of *March;* and if the Full Moon happen upon a *Sunday, Easter* is the *Sunday* after.

Advent Sunday is always the nearest *Sunday* to the thirtieth day of *November*, whether before or after.

The time of *Easter* being found, the other *Festivals* occur as follows:

Septuagesima Sunday is nine weeks before *Easter*.

Ash-Wednesday, or the beginning of *Lent*, is forty-six days before *Easter*.

Palm Sunday, or the beginning of *Passion Week*, is eight days before *Easter*.

Green-Thursday is the *Thursday* before *Easter*.

Good-Friday is the *Friday* before *Easter*.

Ascension-Day is forty days after *Easter*.

Whit-Sunday is seven weeks after *Easter*.

Trinity Sunday is eight weeks after *Easter*.

B.

A Table of the Days on which Easter will fall

From 1860—1899.

Year	Date	Year	Date
1860,	8 April.	1880,	28 March.
1861,	31 March.	1881,	17 April.
1862,	20 April.	1882,	9 "
1863,	5 "	1883,	25 March.
1864,	27 March.	1884,	13 April.
1865,	16 April.	1885,	5 "
1866,	1 "	1886,	25 "
1867,	21 "	1887,	10 "
1868,	12 "	1888,	1 "
1869,	28 March.	1889,	21 "
1870,	17 April.	1890,	6 "
1871,	9 "	1891,	29 March.
1872,	31 March.	1892,	17 April.
1873,	13 April.	1893,	2 "
1874,	5 "	1894,	25 March.
1875,	28 March.	1895,	14 April.
1876,	16 April.	1896,	5 "
1877,	1 "	1897,	18 "
1878,	21 "	1898,	19 "
1879,	13 "	1899,	2 "

FESTIVALS OF THE CHURCH.

C.

A Table of the Moveable Festivals,

ACCORDING TO THE SEVERAL DAYS THAT EASTER CAN POSSIBLY FALL UPON.

Easter.	Sundays after* Epiphany.	Septuagesima Sunday.	Ash-Wednesday.	Ascension-Day.	Whit-Sunday.	Sundays after Trinity.	First Advent Sunday.
March 22	1	Jan. 18	Feb. 4	April 30	May 10	27	Nov. 29
" 23	1	" 19	" 5	May 1	" 11	27	" 30
" 24	1	" 20	" 6	" 2	" 12	27	Dec. 1
" 25	2	" 21	" 7	" 3	" 13	27	" 2
" 26	2	" 22	" 8	" 4	" 14	27	" 3
" 27	2	" 23	" 9	" 5	" 15	26	Nov. 27
" 28	2	" 24	" 10	" 6	" 16	26	" 28
" 29	2	" 25	" 11	" 7	" 17	26	" 29
" 30	2	" 26	" 12	" 8	" 18	26	" 30
" 31	2	" 27	" 13	" 9	" 19	26	Dec. 1
April 1	3	" 28	" 14	" 10	" 20	26	" 2
" 2	3	" 29	" 15	" 11	" 21	26	" 3
" 3	3	" 30	" 16	" 12	" 22	25	Nov. 27
" 4	3	" 31	" 17	" 13	" 23	25	" 28
" 5	3	Feb. 1	" 18	" 14	" 24	25	" 29
" 6	3	" 2	" 19	" 15	" 25	25	" 30
" 7	3	" 3	" 20	" 16	" 26	25	Dec. 1
" 8	4	" 4	" 21	" 17	" 27	25	" 2
" 9	4	" 5	" 22	" 18	" 28	25	" 3
" 10	4	" 6	" 23	" 19	" 29	24	Nov. 27
" 11	4	" 7	" 24	" 20	" 30	24	" 28
" 12	4	" 8	" 25	" 21	" 31	24	" 29
" 13	4	" 9	" 26	" 22	June 1	24	" 30
" 14	4	" 10	" 27	" 23	" 2	24	Dec. 1
" 15	5	" 11	" 28	" 24	" 3	24	" 2
" 16	5	" 12	March 1	" 25	" 4	24	" 3
" 17	5	" 13	" 2	" 26	" 5	23	Nov. 27
" 18	5	" 14	" 3	" 27	" 6	23	" 28
" 19	5	" 15	" 4	" 28	" 7	23	" 29
" 20	5	" 16	" 5	" 29	" 8	23	" 30
" 21	5	" 17	" 6	" 30	" 9	23	Dec. 1
" 22	6	" 18	" 7	" 31	" 10	23	" 2
" 23	6	" 19	" 8	June 1	" 11	23	" 3
" 24	6	" 20	" 9	" 2	" 12	22	Nov. 27
" 25	6	" 21	" 10	" 3	" 13	22	" 28

* In a Leap Year, the number of Sundays after Epiphany is the same as if Easter had fallen one day later than it really does; and Septuagesima Sunday and Ash-Wednesday fall one day later than that given in the Table, unless the Table gives some day in March for Ash-Wednesday: for in that case the day in the Table is right.

Te Deum Laudamus.

We praise thee, O God; we acknowledge thee to be the Lord.
All the earth doth worship thee, the Father everlasting.
To thee all angels cry aloud,—the heavens and all the powers therein.
To thee Cherubim and Seraphim continually do cry,
Holy, holy, holy, Lord God of Sabaoth!
Heaven and earth are full of the majesty of thy glory.
The glorious company of the apostles praise thee.
The goodly fellowship of the prophets praise thee.
The noble army of the martyrs praise thee.
The holy Church throughout the world doth acknowledge thee,
The Father of an infinite majesty:
Thine adorable, true, and only Son;
Also the Holy Ghost, the Comforter.
Thou art the King of glory, O Christ.
Thou art the everlasting Son of the Father!
When thou tookest upon thee to deliver man, thou didst humble thyself to be born of a virgin.
When thou hadst overcome the sharpness of death, thou didst open the kingdom of heaven to all believers.
Thou sittest at the right hand of God, in the glory of the Father.
We believe that thou shalt come to be our Judge.
We therefore pray thee, help thy servants, whom thou hast redeemed with thy precious blood.
Make them to be numbered with thy saints, in glory everlasting.
O Lord, save thy people, and bless thine heritage.
Govern them and lift them up forever.
Day by day we magnify thee;
And we worship thy Name ever, world without end.
Vouchsafe, O Lord, to keep us, this day without sin.
O Lord, have mercy on us, have mercy on us.
O Lord, let thy mercy be upon us, as our trust is in thee.
O Lord, in thee we have trusted; let us never be confounded. Amen.

PART FIRST.

The Order of Divine Service

FOR

SUNDAYS AND FESTIVALS.

I.
The Order of Morning Service.

The Minister standing before the Altar shall say one of the following INTROITS; *after which the Congregation shall say or sing the* GLORIA PATRI, *or the* INTROIT *may be said responsively by the Minister and Congregation, or both the* INTROIT *and the* GLORIA PATRI *may be sung.*

The Introit.

I.

THE Lord is in his holy temple: let all the earth keep silence before him.

R. GLORY BE TO THE FATHER, AND TO THE SON, AND TO THE HOLY GHOST; AS IT WAS IN THE BEGINNING, IS NOW, AND EVER SHALL BE, WORLD WITHOUT END. AMEN.

II. Ps. 67.

GOD be merciful unto us, and bless us;
R. And cause his face to shine upon us.
2. That thy way may be known upon earth.
R. Thy saving health among all nations.
3. Let the people praise thee, O God:
R. Let all the people praise thee.
4. Then shall the earth yield her increase;
R. And God, even our own God, shall bless us.
5. God shall bless us:
R. And all the ends of the earth shall fear him.
GLORY BE TO THE FATHER, AND TO THE SON,
R. AND TO THE HOLY GHOST;
AS IT WAS IN THE BEGINNING, IS NOW, AND EVER SHALL BE,
R. WORLD WITHOUT END. AMEN.

III. Ps. 100.

MAKE a joyful noise unto the Lord, all ye lands:
R. Serve the Lord with gladness, come before his presence with singing.

2. Know ye that the Lord he is God:
   R. It is he that hath made us, and not we ourselves; we are his people, and the sheep of his pasture.
3. Enter into his gates with thanksgiving, and into his courts with praise:
   R. Be thankful unto him, and bless his name.
4. For the Lord is good, his mercy is everlasting;
   R. And his truth endureth to all generations.

GLORY BE TO THE FATHER, AND TO THE SON,
   R. AND TO THE HOLY GHOST;
AS IT WAS IN THE BEGINNING, IS NOW, AND EVER SHALL BE,
   R. WORLD WITHOUT END. AMEN.

IV. Ps. 95.

O COME, let us sing unto the Lord:
   R. Let us make a joyful noise to the Rock of our salvation.
2. Let us come before his presence with thanksgiving:
   R. And make a joyful noise unto him with psalms.
3. For the Lord is a great God,
   R. And a great King above all gods.
4. In his hand are the deep places of the earth:
   R. The strength of the hills is his also.
5. The sea is his, and he made it:
   R. And his hand formed the dry land.
6. O come, let us worship and bow down:
   R. Let us kneel before the Lord our maker.
7. For he is our God:
   R. And we are the people of his pasture, and the sheep of his hand.

GLORY BE TO THE FATHER, AND TO THE SON,
   R. AND TO THE HOLY GHOST;
AS IT WAS IN THE BEGINNING, IS NOW, AND EVER SHALL BE,
   R. WORLD WITHOUT END. AMEN.

V. Ps. 122.

I WAS glad when they said unto me, Let us go into the house of the Lord.
R. Our feet shall stand within thy gates, O Jerusalem.
2. Pray for the peace of Jerusalem:
R. They shall prosper that love thee.
3. Peace be within thy walls,
R. And prosperity within thy palaces.
GLORY BE TO THE FATHER, AND TO THE SON,
R. AND TO THE HOLY GHOST;
AS IT WAS IN THE BEGINNING, IS NOW, AND EVER SHALL BE,
R. WORLD WITHOUT END. AMEN.

VI. Ps. 26.

I WILL wash mine hands in innocency;
R. So will I compass thine altar, O Lord.
2. That I may publish with the voice of thanksgiving,
R. And tell of all thy wondrous works.
3. Lord, I have loved the habitation of thy house,
R. And the place where thine honor dwelleth.
GLORY BE TO THE FATHER, AND TO THE SON,
R. AND TO THE HOLY GHOST;
AS IT WAS IN THE BEGINNING, IS NOW, AND EVER SHALL BE,
R. WORLD WITHOUT END. AMEN.

On Festival-days, the special INTROIT *shall be used instead of a general* INTROIT.

Then the Minister shall say:

The Confession of Sin.

DEARLY Beloved! Let us confess our sins unto God our heavenly Father, and humbly beseech him, in the name of our Lord Jesus Christ, to grant us forgiveness. For if we say that we have no sin, we deceive ourselves, and the truth is not in us. But if we confess our sins, God is faithful and just to forgive us our sins, and to cleanse us from all unrighteousness.

ALMIGHTY and most merciful Father; we poor miserable sinners acknowledge and confess our manifold sins and wickedness, which we, from time to time, most grievously have committed, by thought, word, and deed, against thy Divine Majesty, provoking most justly thy wrath and indignation against us, and deserving at thy hands present and everlasting punishment. But we do earnestly repent, and are heartily sorry for these our misdoings; and we beseech thee, of thy great goodness, to be merciful unto us. Pardon and deliver us from all our sins, for the sake of the holy, innocent, and bitter sufferings and death of thy dear Son, Jesus Christ; and grant us grace ever hereafter to serve and please thee in newness of life, to the honor and glory of thy name, through Jesus Christ our Lord.

Then shall the Congregation say or sing:

The Kyrie.

LORD, have mercy upon us!
Christ, have mercy upon us!
Lord, have mercy upon us!

Instead of the preceding Confession, this may be used:

DEARLY Beloved! The Holy Scriptures declare, that when the wicked man turneth away from his wickedness, and doeth that which is lawful and right, he shall save his soul alive. The sacrifices of God are a broken and a contrite heart. To the Lord belong mercies and forgivenesses, though we have rebelled against him. Let us, therefore, confess our sins unto our Father, with sincere, humble, and obedient hearts, that we may obtain remission of the same, by his infinite goodness and mercy.

ALMIGHTY and most merciful Father, unto whom all hearts are open, and all desires are known, all whose commandments are just, necessary, and good;

we confess unto thee, that we have erred and strayed from thy ways like lost sheep. We have followed too much the devices and desires of our own hearts. We have offended against thy holy laws. We have left undone those things which we ought to have done; and we have done those things which we ought not to have done. But enter not, we beseech thee, into judgment with us; for in thy sight shall no man living be justified. As thou hatest nothing which thou hast made, and desirest not the death of a sinner, but rather that he may turn from his wickedness and live,—have mercy, O Lord, upon us miserable offenders. Spare thou those, O God, who confess their faults. Restore thou those who are truly penitent, according to thy gracious promises, declared unto mankind in Christ Jesus our Lord. And grant, O most merciful Father, that we may hereafter live a godly, righteous, and sober life, to the glory of thy holy name, through thy blessed Son, our Mediator and Redeemer.

Then shall the Congregation say or sing:

The Kyrie.

O GOD the Father in heaven; have mercy upon us! O God the Son, Redeemer of the world; have mercy upon us!
O God the Holy Ghost; have mercy upon us, and grant us thy peace!

Then may the Minister say:

ALMIGHTY God our heavenly Father hath had mercy upon us, and hath given his only Son to die for our sins, and doth for his sake graciously pardon us; he also giveth unto all them that believe in his name the power to become his children, and promises to bestow upon them his Holy Spirit. Praise the Lord; praise ye the name of the Lord.

Then shall the Congregation say:

Amen.

Then shall be sung the GLORIA IN EXCELSIS, *or a hymn of praise.*

The Gloria in Excelsis.

GLORY be to God on high, and on earth peace, good will towards men. We praise thee, we bless thee, we worship thee, we glorify thee, we give thanks to thee for thy great glory, O Lord God, heavenly King, God the Father Almighty.

O Lord, the only begotten Son, Jesus Christ; O Lord God, Lamb of God, Son of the Father, that takest away the sins of the world, have mercy upon us. Thou that takest away the sins of the world, receive our prayer. Thou that sittest at the right hand of God the Father, have mercy upon us.

For thou only art holy, thou only art the Lord; thou only, O Christ, with the Holy Ghost, art most high in the glory of God the Father. Amen.

Then shall the Minister say:

The Lord be with you.

The Congregation shall answer:

And with thy Spirit.

Then shall the Minister say the COLLECT *for the day.* (*See Collects for the Church Year.*)

The Collect.

Then shall the Congregation say:

Amen.

Then shall the Minister read the EPISTLE *for the day, saying:*

Hear the Epistle for the day, written in the ——— chapter of ———, beginning at the ——— verse.

The Epistle.

The EPISTLE *ended, the Congregation shall say:*

Sanctify us, O Lord, through thy truth, thy word is truth.

MORNING SERVICE. 21

Then shall the Minister say:

Hear also the Gospel for the day, written in the ―― chapter of St. ――, beginning at the ―― verse.

The Gospel.

The GOSPEL *ended, the Congregation shall say:*

Praise be to thee, O Christ.

Then shall the Minister and Congregation say the APOSTLES' CREED, *all standing:*

The Apostles' Creed.

I BELIEVE in God the Father Almighty, Maker of heaven and earth.

And in Jesus Christ his only Son, our Lord; Who was conceived by the Holy Ghost, Born of the Virgin Mary; Suffered under Pontius Pilate, Was crucified, dead, and buried; He descended into hell; The third day he rose again from the dead; He ascended into heaven, And sitteth on the right hand of God the Father Almighty; From thence he shall come to judge the quick and the dead.

I believe in the Holy Ghost; The holy Christian Church, the Communion of Saints; The forgiveness of sins; The Resurrection of the body; And the life everlasting. Amen.

Instead of the APOSTLES' CREED *may be said the* NICENE CREED.

I BELIEVE in one God the Father Almighty, Maker of heaven and earth, And of all things visible and invisible.

And in one Lord Jesus Christ, the only-begotten Son of God, Begotten of his Father before all worlds, God of God, Light of Light, very God of very God, Begotten, not made, Being of one substance with the Father, By whom all things were made; Who, for us men, and for our salvation, came down from heaven.

And was incarnate by the Holy Ghost of the Virgin Mary. And was made man; And was crucified also for us under Pontius Pilate. He suffered and was buried; And the third day he rose again, according to the Scriptures; And ascended into heaven, And sitteth on the right hand of the Father; And he shall come again with glory to judge both the quick and the dead, Whose kingdom shall have no end.

And I believe in the Holy Ghost, the Lord and Giver of Life, Who proceedeth from the Father and the Son, Who with the Father and the Son together is worshipped and glorified, Who spake by the Prophets. And I believe one holy Christian and Apostolic Church; I acknowledge one Baptism for the remission of sins; And I look for the Resurrection of the dead, and the Life of the world to come. Amen.

Then shall the Minister offer the GENERAL PRAYER. *He may use the following prayer, or one of the other General Prayers, or any suitable prayer. On Festival-days, the prayer appointed for the day shall be used.*

The Litany.

Minister. LORD, have mercy upon us.
Congregation. Christ, have mercy upon us.
M. Lord, have mercy upon us.
C. O Christ, hear us.
M. O God the Father in heaven.
C. Have mercy upon us.
M. O God the Son, Redeemer of the world;
C. Have mercy upon us.
M. O God the Holy Ghost;
C. Have mercy upon us.
M. Be gracious unto us.
C. Spare us good Lord.
M. Be gracious unto us,
C. Help us, good Lord.
M. From all sin; from all error; from all evil;
C. Good Lord, deliver us.

M. From the crafts and assaults of the devil; from sudden death; from pestilence and famine; from war and bloodshed; from sedition and rebellion; from storms and tempests; from all calamity by fire and water; and from everlasting death;

C. Good Lord, deliver us.

M. By thy holy nativity; by thine agony and bloody sweat; by thy cross and passion; by thy precious death and burial; by thy glorious resurrection and ascension; in the hour of our death, and in the day of judgment;

C. Help us, good Lord.

M. We poor sinners do beseech thee;

C. To hear us, O Lord God.

M. And that it may please thee to rule and govern thy holy Christian Church; to preserve all pastors and ministers of thy Church in the true knowledge and understanding of thy word, and in holiness of life; to put an end to all schisms and causes of offence; to restore all such as have erred, and are deceived; to beat down Satan under our feet; to send faithful laborers into thy harvest; to accompany thy word with thy Spirit and grace; and to comfort and help the weak-hearted and distressed;

C. We beseech thee to hear us, good Lord.

M. That it may please thee to give to all nations peace and concord; to preserve our country from discord and contention; to give us the victory over all thy enemies; to grant to all our rulers wisdom to execute justice, and to maintain truth; and to help all our people to love and fear thee, and diligently to live after thy commandments;

C. We beseech thee to hear us, good Lord.

M. That it may please thee to succor, help, and comfort, all who are in danger, necessity, and tribulation; to preserve all women in the perils of childbirth;

to strengthen and keep all sick persons, and all children; to set free all who are innocently imprisoned; to defend and provide for all widows and orphans; and to have mercy upon all men;

C. We beseech thee to hear us, good Lord.

M. That it may please thee to forgive our enemies, persecutors, and slanderers, and to turn their hearts; to give and preserve to our use the fruits of the earth; and graciously to hear our prayers;

C. We beseech thee to hear us, good Lord.

M. O Lord Jesus Christ, Son of God;

C. We beseech thee to hear us.

M. O Lamb of God, who takest away the sins of the world;

C. Have mercy upon us.

M. O Lamb of God, who takest away the sins of the world;

C. Have mercy upon us.

M. O Lamb of God, who takest away the sins of the world;

C. Grant us thy peace.

M. O Christ, hear us: Lord, have mercy upon us.

C. Christ, have mercy upon us.

M. Lord, have mercy upon us.

C. Amen.

Then shall the Minister say the LITANY COLLECTS *here following, and at the close of each the Congregation shall say,* AMEN.

M. O Lord, deal not with us after our sins.

C. Neither reward us according to our iniquities.

Minister.

ALMIGHTY and most merciful God, our heavenly Father, who desirest not the death of a sinner, but rather that he should be converted and live; we most earnestly beseech thee, to turn from us those punishments, which by our sins we most justly have deserved, and to grant us grace ever hereafter to serve thee in holiness and pureness of living; through Jesus Christ our Lord. *Amen.*

ALMIGHTY and everlasting God, who by thy Holy Spirit dost govern and sanctify the whole Christian Church; favorably hear our prayer, and mercifully grant, that by thy grace all the members of the same may serve thee, in true faith; through Jesus Christ thy Son our Lord. *Amen.*

O GOD, merciful Father, who despisest not the sighing of a contrite heart, nor the desire of such as are sorrowful; mercifully assist our prayers which we make before thee in all our troubles and adversities, whensoever they oppress us; and graciously hear us, that those evils which the craft or subtilty of the devil or man worketh against us, may, by thy good providence, be brought to nought; that we thy servants, being hurt by no persecutions, may evermore give thanks unto thee in thy holy Church; through Jesus Christ thy Son our Lord.* *Amen.*

ALMIGHTY God, who knowest us to be set in the midst of so many and great dangers, that by reason of the frailty of our nature we cannot always stand upright; grant to us such strength and protection, as may support us in all dangers, and carry us through all temptations; through Jesus Christ thy Son our Lord. *Amen.*

---

* This Collect, and the one next following, are found in the Book of Common Prayer of the Protestant Episcopal Church; the same is true of a number of the Sunday, General, and Special Collects, and results from the fact, that both the German from which this work is translated, and the English of the Book of Common Prayer, are translations of the same ancient Latin Collect. The great excellence of the translation renders a new one unnecessary.

S PARE us, O Lord, and mercifully forgive us our sins, and though by our continual transgressions we have merited thy punishments, graciously look upon us; and grant that all those evils which we most justly have deserved, may be turned from us, and overruled to our everlasting good; through Jesus Christ thy Son our Lord. *Amen.*

Then shall be sung a suitable Hymn, during which time the Minister shall go into the pulpit, and the singing ended, he shall preach:

The Sermon.

Then shall the Minister and the Congregation say:

The Lord's Prayer.

OUR Father, who art in heaven; Hallowed be thy name; Thy kingdom come; Thy will be done on earth, as it is in heaven; Give us this day our daily bread; And forgive us our trespasses, as we forgive those who trespass against us; And lead us not into temptation; But deliver us from evil; For thine is the kingdom, and the power, and the glory, for ever and ever. Amen.

Then shall a Hymn be sung, and after that the Minister, standing at the Altar, shall pronounce:

The Benediction.

The Lord bless thee, and keep thee;

The Lord make his face shine upon thee, and be gracious unto thee.

The Lord lift up his countenance upon thee, and give thee peace.

The Congregation shall say:

Amen.

The Holy Communion.

The Minister, standing before the Altar, shall say:
The Lord be with you.
The Congregation shall answer:
And with thy spirit.
Minister.
Lift up your hearts.
Congregation.
We lift them up unto the Lord.
Minister.
Let us give thanks unto our Lord God.
Congregation.
It is meet and right so to do.
Minister.

IT is truly meet, right, and salutary, that we should at all times, and in all places, give thanks unto thee, O Lord, Holy Father, Almighty Everlasting God, through Jesus Christ, thy dear Son, our Lord and Saviour. Therefore with Angels and Archangels, and with all the company of heaven, we laud and magnify thy glorious name; evermore praising thee, and saying:

Here shall the Minister and Congregation say or sing:

The Sanctus.

HOLY, holy, holy, Lord God of Sabaoth;
Heaven and earth are full of thy glory;
Hosanna in the highest.
Blessed is he that cometh in the name of the Lord.
Hosanna in the highest.

Proper Prefaces.

On Christmas-day, after the words, Everlasting God:

FOR in the mystery of the Word made flesh, thou hast given us a new revelation of thy glory; that seeing thee in the person of thy Son, we may be drawn to the love of those things which are not seen. Therefore with Angels, &c.

During Lent, after the words, Lord and Saviour:

WHO for the redemption of our sinful race was lifted up upon the cross; to the end that where death began, there also life might be restored; that he who overcame at the tree of the garden should also be overcome on the tree of the cross. Therefore with Angels, &c.

On Easter-Day, after the words, Everlasting God:

BUT chiefly are we bound to praise thee for the glorious Resurrection of thy Son Jesus Christ our Lord: for he is the very Paschal Lamb, which was offered for us, and hath taken away the sin of the world; who by his death hath destroyed death, and by his rising to life again, hath restored to us everlasting life. Therefore with Angels, &c.

On Whit-Sunday, after the words, Lord and Saviour:

WHO ascending above the heavens, and sitting at thy right hand, poured out on this day the Holy Spirit, as he had promised, upon the chosen disciples; whereat the whole earth rejoices with exceeding joy. Therefore with Angels, &c.

On Trinity Sunday, after the words, Everlasting God:

WHO with thine only begotten Son, and the Holy Ghost, art one God, one Lord; not one only Person, but three Persons in one Substance. For that which we believe, according to thy revelation, of the glory of the Father, the same we believe of the Son, and of the Holy Ghost, without any difference or inequality. And in the confession of the only true God, we worship the Trinity in Person, and the Unity in Substance, of Majesty co-equal. Therefore with Angels, &c.

Then shall the Minister say this EXHORTATION:

DEARLY Beloved in the Lord! Forasmuch as we purpose to come to the Holy Supper of our Lord, wherein he giveth us his body to eat and his blood to drink, in order to strengthen and confirm our faith in him, it becomes us diligently to examine ourselves, as St. Paul the Apostle exhorteth: "Let a man examine himself, and so let him eat of that bread and drink of that cup." For this holy Sacrament is instituted as a special means to strengthen and comfort the troubled conscience of those who confess their sins, and who hunger and thirst after righteousness.

Therefore, whoso eateth of this bread, and drinketh of this cup, firmly believing the words of Christ, dwelleth in Christ, and Christ in him, and he hath eternal life. Let us also obey his command: "This do in remembrance of me;" showing his death, that he was delivered for our offences, and raised again for our justification, and rendering unto him most hearty thanks for the innumerable benefits procured unto us by the same, take up our cross and follow him, and love one another even as he hath loved us. For we are all *one* bread, and *one* body, even as we eat of *one* bread, and drink of one cup.

The Consecration.

GLORY be to thee, O Lord Jesus Christ, thou almighty and everlasting Son of the Father, that by the sacrifice of thyself upon the cross, offered up once for all, thou didst perfect them that are sanctified, and didst institute and ordain, as a memorial and seal thereof, thy Holy Supper, in which thou givest us thy body to eat, and thy blood to drink, that being in thee, even as thou art in us, we may have eternal life, and be raised up at the last day. Most merciful and exalted Redeemer, we humbly confess that we are not worthy of the least of all the mercies, and of all the truth, which thou hast showed unto us, and that by reason of our sins, we are too impure and weak worthily to receive thy saving gifts. Sanctify us therefore, we beseech thee, in our bodies and souls, by thy Holy Spirit, and thus fit and prepare us to come to thy Supper, to the glory of thy grace, and to our own eternal good. And in whatsoever, through weakness, we do fail and come short, in true repentance and sorrow on account of our sins, in living faith and trust in thy merits, and in an earnest purpose to amend our sinful lives, do thou graciously supply and grant, out of the fullness of the merits of thy bitter sufferings and death; to the end that we, who even in this present world desire to enjoy thee, our only comfort and Saviour, in the Holy Sacrament, may at last see thee face to face in thy heavenly kingdom, and dwell with thee, and with all thy saints, for ever and ever. *Amen.*

Then the Minister, turning toward the Altar, shall say:

OUR Father, who art in heaven; hallowed be thy name; thy kingdom come; thy will be done on earth, as it is in heaven; give us this day our daily bread; and forgive us our trespasses, as we forgive those who trespass against us; and lead us not into temptation; but deliver us from evil; for thine is the kingdom, and the power, and the glory, for ever and ever. Amen.

Our Lord Jesus Christ, in the night in which he was betrayed, took bread; (*a*) and when he had given thanks, he brake

(*a*) Here he is to take the plate with the bread in his hand.

and gave it to his disciples, saying, Take, eat; this is my body, which is given for you; this do in remembrance of me.

After the same manner, also, he took the cup,(*b*) when he had supped, and when he had given thanks, he gave it to them, saying, Drink ye all of it; this cup is the New Testament in my blood, which is shed for you, and for many, for the remission of sins; this do, as oft as ye drink it, in remembrance of me. *(b) Here he is to take the cup in his hand.*

Then shall be sung the AGNUS DEI, *or some other sacramental Hymn.*

The Agnus Dei.

O CHRIST, thou Lamb of God, that takest away the sins of the world, have mercy upon us!

O Christ, thou Lamb of God, that takest away the sins of the world, have mercy upon us!

O Christ, thou Lamb of God, that takest away the sins of the world, grant us thy peace. Amen.

At the close of the AGNUS DEI, *or such other sacramental Hymn as is used, the* DISTRIBUTION *shall begin.*

When the Minister giveth the Bread, he shall say:

TAKE, eat, this is the body of our Lord Jesus Christ which was given for you; may it strengthen and preserve you in the true faith unto everlasting life.

When he giveth the Cup, he shall say:

TAKE and drink, this is the blood of our Lord Jesus Christ, which was shed for you and for many for the remission of sins; may it strengthen and preserve you in the true faith unto everlasting life.

When all have communicated, the Minister shall reverently place upon the Altar what remaineth of the consecrated elements, covering the same.

Then may be said or sung:

The Nunc Dimittis.

LORD, now lettest thou thy servant depart in peace, according to thy word:

For mine eyes have seen thy salvation, which thou hast prepared before the face of all people;

A light to lighten the Gentiles, and the glory of thy people Israel.

Glory be to the Father, and to the Son, and to the Holy Ghost; as it was in the beginning, is now, and ever shall be, world without end.   Amen.

Then shall be said:

The Thanksgiving.

Minister.

O give thanks unto the Lord, for he is good:

Congregation.

And his mercy endureth for ever.

Minister.

ALMIGHTY God, our heavenly Father, we most heartily thank thee that thou hast again vouchsafed to feed us with the most precious body and blood of thy dear Son, our Saviour Jesus Christ; and we humbly beseech thee, graciously to strengthen us, through this holy sacrament, in faith toward thee, in charity toward one another, and in the blessed hope of everlasting life, through Jesus Christ, thy dear Son our Lord, who liveth and reigneth with Thee, in the unity of the Holy Spirit, world without end.

Congregation.

Amen.   Amen.

Minister.

Blessed be the name of the Lord.

Congregation.

From now, henceforth, and forever.

Minister.

The Lord bless thee, and keep thee;

The Lord make his face shine upon thee, and be gracious unto thee.

The Lord lift up his countenance upon thee, and give thee peace.

Congregation.

Amen.

II.

The Order of Evening Service.

If there is but one service on the Lord's Day, the Order of Morning Service may be used whenever that service is held. But where in addition to the Morning Service there is also an Evening Service, the following Order may be observed.

The Minister shall begin with the Apostolic Salutation: "Grace be unto you, and peace, from God our Father, and from the Lord Jesus Christ;" Or this sentence: "O Lord, open thou my lips, and my mouth shall show forth thy praise;" Or this: "O Lord, abide with us, for it is evening, and the day is far spent." Then shall follow :

1. A Hymn.
2. Prayer.
3. The Scripture Lessons. The Scriptures ended, the Minister shall say : " Sanctify us, O Lord, through thy truth, thy word is truth;" Or this : " Blessed be the name of the Lord, from this time forth, and forevermore."
4. The Sermon.
5. The Lord's Prayer, or one of the Collects for the close of the Service.
6. A Hymn.
7. The Benediction.

Where a more extended Service is desired, the Order of Morning Service may be followed, substituting the Scripture Lessons for the Epistle and Gospel for the day, and omitting portions, at the discretion of the Minister.

III.
The Festival Introits.

Advent.

HOSANNA to the Son of David;
  R. Blessed is he that cometh in the name of the Lord.
2. Rejoice greatly, O daughter of Zion;
  R. Shout, O daughter of Jerusalem;
3. Behold, thy king cometh unto thee;
  R. He is just, and having salvation.
4. Show me thy ways, O Lord;
  R. Teach me thy paths.
GLORY BE TO THE FATHER, AND TO THE SON,
  R. AND TO THE HOLY GHOST;
AS IT WAS IN THE BEGINNING, IS NOW, AND EVER SHALL BE,
  R. WORLD WITHOUT END. AMEN.

II.

LIFT up your heads, O ye gates; and be ye lift up, ye everlasting doors;
  R. And the King of Glory shall come in.
2. Who is this King of Glory?
  R. The Lord, strong and mighty, the Lord mighty in battle.
3. Lift up your heads, O ye gates; even lift them up, ye everlasting doors;
  R. And the King of Glory shall come in.
4. Who is this King of Glory?
  R. The Lord of hosts, he is the King of Glory.
GLORY BE TO THE FATHER, AND TO THE SON,
  R. AND TO THE HOLY GHOST;
AS IT WAS IN THE BEGINNING, IS NOW, AND EVER SHALL BE,
  R. WORLD WITHOUT END. AMEN.

Christmas.

BLESSED be the Lord God of Israel;
 R. For he hath visited, and redeemed his people;
2. And hath raised up an horn of salvation for us,
 R. In the house of his servant David;
3. As he spake by the mouth of his holy Prophets,
 R. Which have been since the world began;
4. That we should be saved from our enemies,
 R. And from the hand of all that hate us.
GLORY BE TO THE FATHER, AND TO THE SON,
 R. AND TO THE HOLY GHOST;
AS IT WAS IN THE BEGINNING, IS NOW, AND EVER SHALL BE,
 R. WORLD WITHOUT END. AMEN.

Epiphany.

OUR help is in the name of the Lord,
 R. Who made heaven and earth.
2. Declare his glory among the heathen,
 R. His wonders among all people.
3. The people which sat in darkness, saw a great light;
 R. And to them which sat in the region and shadow of death, light is sprung up.
GLORY BE TO THE FATHER, AND TO THE SON, AND TO THE HOLY GHOST;
 R. AS IT WAS IN THE BEGINNING, IS NOW, AND EVER SHALL BE, WORLD WITHOUT END. AMEN.

Good Friday.

BEHOLD the Lamb of God;
 R. Which taketh away the sin of the world!
2. Surely he hath borne our griefs;
 R. And carried our sorrows.
3. He was wounded for our transgressions;
 R. He was bruised for our iniquities.

4. All we like sheep have gone astray;
   R. And the Lord hath laid on him the iniquity of us all.

   (The Gloria Patri is omitted on this day.)

Easter.

THE Lord is risen, and hath appeared unto Simon. Hallelujah!
   R. The Lord is risen indeed. Hallelujah!
2. Why seek ye the living among the dead? Hallelujah!
   R. He is not here, he is risen; Hallelujah!
3. Thou hast crowned him with glory and honor; Hallelujah!
   R. Thou madest him to have dominion over the works of thy hand. Hallelujah!

GLORY BE TO THE FATHER, AND TO THE SON,
   R. AND TO THE HOLY GHOST;
AS IT WAS IN THE BEGINNING, IS NOW, AND EVER SHALL BE,
   R. WORLD WITHOUT END. AMEN.

Ascension.

YE men of Galilee, why stand ye gazing up into heaven?
   R. Hallelujah!
2. He shall so come in like manner as ye have seen him go into heaven.
   R. Hallelujah! Hallelujah! Hallelujah!
3. O clap your hands all ye people,
   R. Shout unto God with the voice of triumph.

GLORY BE TO THE FATHER, AND TO THE SON, AND TO THE HOLY GHOST;
   R. AS IT WAS IN THE BEGINNING, IS NOW, AND EVER SHALL BE, WORLD WITHOUT END. AMEN.

Pentecost, or Whitsunday.

THE whole earth is full of the Spirit of the Lord.
  R. Hallelujah!
2. I will pour water upon him that is thirsty;
  R. And floods upon the dry ground.
3. I will pour my Spirit upon thy seed;
  R. And my blessing upon thine offspring.
4. God is the Lord, which has showed us light;
  R. Bind the sacrifice with cords, even unto the horns of the altar.

GLORY BE TO THE FATHER, AND TO THE SON, AND TO THE HOLY GHOST;
  R. AS IT WAS IN THE BEGINNING, IS NOW, AND EVER SHALL BE, WORLD WITHOUT END. AMEN.

Trinity Sunday.

HOLY, holy, holy, is the Lord God of Hosts;
  R. The whole earth is full of his glory.
2. There are three that bear record in heaven, the Father, the Word, and the Holy Ghost;
  R. And these three are one.
3. Of him, and through him, and to him are all things;
  R. To whom be glory, for ever. Amen.

GLORY BE TO THE FATHER, AND TO THE SON,
  R. AND TO THE HOLY GHOST;
AS IT WAS IN THE BEGINNING, IS NOW, AND EVER SHALL BE,
  R. WORLD WITHOUT END. AMEN.

The Festival of the Reformation.

THE Lord our God be with us;
  R. As he was with our fathers.
2. Do good in thy good pleasure unto Zion;
  R. Build thou the walls of Jerusalem.
3. Thy testimonies are very sure;

R. Holiness becometh thine house, O Lord, for ever.

GLORY BE TO THE FATHER, AND TO THE SON, AND TO THE HOLY GHOST;

R. AS IT WAS IN THE BEGINNING, IS NOW, AND EVER SHALL BE, WORLD WITHOUT END. AMEN.

IV.
The Collects for the Sundays and Festivals of the Church-Year.

The First Sunday in Advent.

O LORD God our heavenly Father, we give thanks unto thee that for the consolation of us poor sinners thou hast ordained and sent thy Son Jesus Christ to be a King and Saviour, that he might redeem his people from their sins and save them from everlasting death; and we pray thee: so enlighten, rule and direct us by thy Holy Spirit, that we may heartily receive him as our King and Saviour, cleave to him alone, and by steadfast confidence in him, obtain everlasting life; through the same thy Son, who liveth and reigneth with thee and the Holy Spirit, for ever and ever. *Amen.*[*]

Or this:

ALMIGHTY and everlasting God, who by thy grace dost permit us to begin a new Church-Year; we beseech thee: pour out thy Holy Spirit upon thy Church, that thy word may increase and abound among us, that it may be preached with all boldness; that so thy holy Church may be preserved and built up, and that we, serving thee with steadfast faith, may persevere in the confession of thy name unto the end; through Jesus Christ, thy dear Son, our Lord. Amen.

The Epistle: Rom. xiii. 11–14
The Gospel: Mat. xxi. 1–9.

---

[*] Here, and whenever the word AMEN is printed in Italics, it is to be said aloud by the Congregation.

The Second Sunday in Advent.

ALMIGHTY God our Lord; we pray thee: grant us grace that now in the time of this mortal life, in which thy Son Jesus Christ came to redeem us, we may put off the works of darkness and put on the armor of light; so that at the last day when he shall come again in his glorious Majesty to judge both the quick and the dead, we may rise to life eternal; through him who liveth and reigneth with thee and the Holy Ghost, for ever and ever. *Amen.*

The Epistle: Rom. xv. 4–13.
The Gospel: Luke xxi. 25–36.

The Third Sunday in Advent.

O LORD Jesus Christ, who at thy first coming didst send thy messenger to prepare thy way before thee; we beseech thee: raise up unto thy Church faithful ministers of thy divine word, and grant that those whom thou hast appointed to be stewards of thy mysteries may like him make ready thy way by turning the hearts of the disobedient to the wisdom of the just. And excite within us all, a sincere desire for thy salvation, that we may with willing hearts receive and treasure up thy saving word, and thus, when thou shalt come again to judge the world, we may be found an acceptable people in thy sight, who livest and reignest, for ever and ever. *Amen.*

The Epistle: 1 Cor. iv. 1–5.
The Gospel: Mat. xi. 2–10.

The Fourth Sunday in Advent.

O LORD God, our heavenly Father, we give thanks to thee with our whole heart, that thou didst institute the holy Sacrament of Baptism, and didst also permit us to come to the same, in which, for Jesus

Christ's sake, thou grantest us forgiveness of sins and everlasting life; and we pray thee: prepare our hearts, in this time of grace, by thy holy Spirit, for the indwelling of thy dear Son, that when he would take up his abode within us, we may receive him with joy, and in blessed fellowship with him, may evermore praise thee with joyful lips, as our God and Father; through Jesus Christ our Lord. *Amen.*

The Epistle: Phil. iv. 4–7.
The Gospel: John i. 19–28.

Christmas-Day.

O LORD God, our heavenly Father, we thank thee that of thy great goodness and mercy, thou hast caused thine only-begotten Son to become partaker of our flesh and blood, that we through him might be redeemed from sin and everlasting death; and we pray thee: enlighten our hearts, that we may be truly thankful to thee for his gracious incarnation and birth, that we may be comforted by the same in all time of tribulation and temptation, and in the end be saved with an everlasting salvation; through the same, thy dear Son, Jesus Christ our Lord. *Amen.*

The Epistle: Tit. ii. 11–14.
Or: Isa. ix. 2–7.
The Gospel: Luke ii. 1–14.

Second Christmas-Day, or St. Stephen's Day.

O MOST merciful and gracious God, who, moved by paternal love, didst send thy Son into this world, and at his birth didst cause to be published by the heavenly hosts, peace on earth and good will toward men; grant us now thy grace and help us, that we may be made partakers of these glorious gifts, and may magnify and praise thee therefor; until in heaven, with all the angels and the redeemed, we shall sing Hallelujah to thee for ever and ever; through Jesus Christ, thy Son, our Lord. *Amen.*

Or:

ALMIGHTY God, our heavenly Father; grant us, we beseech thee, thy Holy Spirit, that in all our sufferings here upon earth for the testimony of thy truth, we may steadfastly look up to heaven, and by faith behold the glory which shall be revealed; that we being filled with thy grace, may learn to love and pray for our enemies and persecutors, and in the end obtain a glorious inheritance on high; through Jesus Christ thy Son, who liveth and reigneth with thee, in the unity of the Holy Spirit, world without end. *Amen.*

The Epistle: Tit. iii. 4–7.
Or: Acts vi. 8—vii. 1, 51–59.
The Gospel: Luke ii. 15–20.

The Sunday after Christmas-Day.

ALMIGHTY and everlasting God, who hast set thy beloved Son Jesus Christ for the fall and rising again of many in Israel, and for a sign which shall be spoken against, that the thoughts of many hearts may be revealed; we pray thee: so govern us by thy good Spirit, that we may not be offended in him our only Saviour, but by the preaching of his word may learn to see our own hearts as thou seest them, and may be awakened by his grace out of the slumber of sin, and arise to true repentance and living faith; for the sake of the same, thy dear Son our Lord. *Amen.*

The Epistle: Gal. iv. 1–7.
The Gospel: Luke ii. 33–40.

The Close of the Year: (*Sylvester Evening.*)

ALMIGHTY God, most gracious Father, from whom we do constantly receive all manner of good, which we have in no wise merited, we give thee thanks that in the year which is now drawing to a close, thou hast so graciously and mightily protected us, and hast bestowed upon us so many blessings both temporal and spiritual; and we pray thee: enable us by thy Spirit, with true faith, to acknowledge all these thy benefits, that so we may evermore thank and praise thee for thy goodness and mercy; through our Lord Jesus Christ, who liveth and reigneth with thee and the Holy Ghost, true God, world without end. *Amen.*

The Epistle: 2 Tim. iv. 1-8.
The Gospel: Luke xii. 35-40.

The Circumcision of Christ, and New Year's Day.

O LORD God, heavenly Father, we give thanks to thee that thou hast made thy dearly beloved and only-begotten Son obedient to the law, that he might redeem them that were under the law from the curse; we beseech thee: enlighten our hearts by thy Holy Spirit, that when our consciences accuse us of sin, we may be comforted by his obedience, may walk during this year in newness of life, and at last inherit everlasting salvation; through the same thy Son, who liveth and reigneth with thee, in the unity of the Holy Spirit, for ever and ever. *Amen.*

Or:

ALMIGHTY God, our heavenly Father, we give thee humble and hearty thanks that during the past year thou hast preserved us from all evil, hast bestowed upon us all manner of good, and dost permit us to enter upon a new year; and we pray: that it may please thee mercifully to crown the same with thy goodness, to bless us and our households with thy heavenly gifts, and to grant and preserve unto us whatsoever is necessary for our bodily wants, to avert from us all calamities and evils, and to make this to be unto us a blessed, peaceful, and happy year; for the sake of Jesus Christ, thy dear Son, our only Saviour. *Amen.*

The Epistle: Gal. iii. 23–29.
The Gospel: Luke ii 21.

The Epiphany, or the Manifestation of Christ to the Gentiles.

O LORD God, heavenly Father, who by the leading of a star didst manifest thy only-begotten Son to the Gentiles; we give thee hearty thanks that by the blood of Christ, thou hast made us nigh who were in times past Gentiles in the flesh, being aliens from the commonwealth of Israel, and strangers from the covenants of promise, and hast made us fellow-citizens with the saints, and of the household of God; and we pray thee: enlighten us by thy Holy Spirit, that we may realize this thy grace, may comfort ourselves with the same in true faith, and by a holy conversation, show forth the praises of him who hath called us out of darkness into his marvellous light; through Jesus Christ, thy dear Son, our Lord. *Amen.*

The Epistle: Isaiah lx. 1–6.
The Gospel: Mat. ii. 1–12.

The First Sunday after Epiphany.

O LORD Jesus Christ, who wast seated in the temple in the midst of the doctors, both hearing them and asking them questions; so rule us by thy Holy Spirit, that we, following thy example, may love the habitation of thy house, and the place where thy honor dwelleth, may diligently seek the same with our children, hearing thy word with gladness and faithfully keeping it to the saving of our souls; O thou who livest and reignest with the Father and the Holy Spirit, for ever and ever. *Amen.*

The Epistle: Rom. xii. 1–6.
The Gospel: Luke ii. 41–52.

The Second Sunday after Epiphany.

O LORD God, our heavenly Father, who by signs and wonders didst show forth the glory of thy dear Son Jesus Christ during his sojourn on earth; grant us we beseech thee, thy Holy Spirit, the Spirit of Glory, that we through his help may believe in Jesus Christ, may know the riches of his glorious grace, and be clothed in our inward man with the manifold gifts of the same; through thy dear Son our Lord. *Amen.*

The Epistle: Rom. xii. 7–16.
The Gospel: John ii. 1–11.

The Third Sunday after Epiphany.

O LORD Jesus Christ, thou Comforter and Helper of all them that are in trouble, as we by reason of our sins and infirmities are subject to many diseases and sufferings; we pray thee: give us steadfast faith, that in all our sufferings and tribulations we may take refuge in thee, and experiencing thy help, may give thanks, now and evermore, unto thee, who with the Father and the Holy Ghost livest and reignest, one God, for ever and ever. *Amen.*

The Epistle: Rom. xii. 17–21.
The Gospel: Mat. viii. 1–13.

The Fourth Sunday after Epiphany.

O GOD, who knowest us to be set in the midst of so many and great dangers, that by reason of the frailty of our nature we cannot always stand upright;

grant to us such strength and protection, as may support us in all dangers, and carry us through all temptations; through Jesus Christ our Lord. *Amen.*

The Epistle: Rom. xiii. 8–10.
The Gospel: Mat. viii. 23–27.

The Fifth Sunday after Epiphany.

O LORD, we beseech thee to keep thy Church and household continually in thy true religion; that they who do lean only upon the hope of thy heavenly grace may evermore be defended by thy mighty power; through Jesus Christ our Lord, who liveth and reigneth with thee and the Holy Ghost, for ever and ever. *Amen.*

The Epistle: Col. iii. 12–17.
The Gospel: Mat. xiii. 24–30.

The Sixth Sunday after Epiphany.

ALMIGHTY and everlasting God, whose dear Son Jesus Christ was transfigured before the eyes of his brethren; we pray thee: show forth his glory in our hearts also by thy Holy Spirit, to the end that we may know him as the true light of our life, and cleave to him with sincere devotion, that we may give heed with all diligence to his word, and be followers of him, that thus we may be transformed by his grace into his image from glory to glory; for the sake of our Lord and Saviour. *Amen.*

The Epistle: 2 Pet. i. 16–21.
Or: Col. iii. 18—iv. 1.
The Gospel: Mat. xvii. 1–9.

The Third Sunday before Lent. Septuagesima.

O LORD God, our heavenly Father, we give thanks unto thee that thou hast called us into thy Church, thine earthly vineyard; and we pray thee:

grant us thy Holy Spirit, that we may cheerfully obey that call, and be found as faithful laborers, so that when the evening of our day on earth has come, we may receive through grace the reward of everlasting life; through Jesus Christ, thy dear Son, our Lord. *Amen.*

The Epistle: 1 Cor. ix. 24—x. 5.
The Gospel: Mat. xx. 1–16.

The Second Sunday before Lent. Sexagesima.

ALMIGHTY God, our heavenly Father, who dost so graciously sow the seed of thy divine word in our hearts; grant that it may fall upon good ground, and that we, gladly hearing thy word, and sincerely believing it, may treasure it up in good and honest hearts, that so we may bear much fruit to the honor of thy name and to our own salvation; through Jesus Christ, thy dear Son, our Lord. *Amen.*

The Epistle: 2 Cor. xi. 19—xii. 9.
The Gospel: Luke viii. 4–15.

The Sunday before Lent. Quinquagesima, or Esto Mihi.

O LORD Jesus Christ, who on thy way to Jerusalem to be crucified, didst open the eyes of the blind, and didst proclaim unto thy disciples everlasting redemption through thy death; we pray thee: cause by thy Holy Spirit the light of faith to shine upon us, that we may clearly behold the fullness of that love wherewith thou hast loved us even unto death, and may obtain grace in all things to follow in thy footsteps; who with the Father and the Holy Spirit livest and reignest, for ever and ever. *Amen.*

The Epistle: 1 Cor. xiii. 1–13.
The Gospel: Luke xviii. 31–43.

The First Sunday in Lent. *Invocavit.*

ALMIGHTY and everlasting God, our heavenly Father, who didst give thy Son to suffer for us the painful death of the cross, that thou mightest remove from us the power of the enemy; grant that the bitter sufferings of thy dear Son may so move our hearts, that we may seek and obtain the forgiveness of our sins and everlasting redemption; through the same thy Son, Jesus Christ our Lord. *Amen.*

Or:

O LORD Jesus Christ, who didst fast forty days and forty nights in the wilderness, and didst overcome all the temptations of the devil; we thank thee, that for our salvation, thou wast in all points tempted like as we are, yet without sin, and as our merciful High Priest canst be touched with the feeling of our infirmities; and we pray thee: give us grace steadfastly to resist the allurements of sin, that the lusts of our flesh being subdued to the Spirit, we may ever obey thy godly motions in righteousness and true holiness, to thy honor and glory, who livest and reignest with the Father and the Holy Ghost, one God, world without end. *Amen.*

The Epistle: 2 Cor. vi. 1–10.
The Gospel: Mat. iv. 1–11.

The Second Sunday in Lent. *Reminiscere.*

ALMIGHTY and everlasting God, we give thanks to thee, that for our sake, thy dear Son fought the good fight of faith, and learned obedience through suffering, that being made perfect he might become the author of eternal salvation unto all them that obey him; and we pray thee: grant us thy Holy Spirit, that we, being truly obedient to his word, may hold fast our confidence in his grace amid all dangers and temptations, and so in all things be more than conquerors through him that loved us, Jesus Christ, thy Son, our Lord. *Amen.*

The Epistle: 1 Thess. iv. 1–7.
The Gospel: Mat. xv. 21–28.

The Third Sunday in Lent. Oculi.

ALMIGHTY and everlasting God, who by the holy and precious suffering and death of thy dear Son hast destroyed the works of the devil, and spoiled principalities and powers; we most heartily thank thee for this thy goodness and mercy; and we humbly pray thee: grant us thy Holy Spirit, that with true faith we may lay hold on the victory of our Lord Jesus Christ, and thus, being made free from the power of Satan and of darkness, we may serve thee alone, and be thine in life and in death; through the same thy Son, Jesus Christ our Lord. *Amen.*

The Epistle: Ephes. v. 1–9.
The Gospel: Luke xi. 14–28.

The Fourth Sunday in Lent. Laetare.

O LORD Jesus Christ, who with a few loaves and fishes didst wonderfully feed the thousands; we pray thee: grant us grace to be content with whatever things thy goodness bestows upon us, help us rightly to use thy manifold gifts, and at all times with filial gratitude to give thanks to thee, who livest and reignest with the Father and the Holy Spirit, for ever and ever. *Amen.*

The Epistle: Gal. iv. 21–31.
The Gospel: John vi. 1–15.

The Fifth Sunday in Lent. Judica.

ALMIGHTY and everlasting God, who didst cause thy dear Son for our sake to endure such contradiction of sinners; we pray thee: so rule our hearts by thy Holy Spirit, that we being truly obedient to his commands, may always be acceptable before him, and looking diligently to him in faith, may not become weary or negligent in the profession of the truth, that so, keeping his word we may never see death; through the same Jesus Christ our Lord, who liveth and reigneth with thee and the Holy Spirit, ever one God, world without end. *Amen.*

The Epistle: Heb. ix. 11–15.
The Gospel: John viii. 46–59.

The Sixth Sunday in Lent. Palmarum.

ALMIGHTY and everlasting God, who hast led thy dear Son Jesus Christ through sufferings and death to thine eternal glory, and hast exalted him at thy right hand to be Lord of Lords and King of Kings; we beseech thee: grant us thy good Spirit, that with willing hearts we may receive him as our King, follow his example in true humility, that being made perfect through sufferings, we may enter into eternal glory; through the same thy Son, Jesus Christ our Lord. *Amen.*

The Epistle: Phil. ii. 5–11.
Or: 1 Cor. xi. 23–32.
The Gospel: Mat. xxi. 1–9.

Thursday before Easter.

ALMIGHTY God, our heavenly Father, we give thee humble and hearty thanks that thou hast given thy dear Son to die for us, that he might not only bear our sins and make atonement for us upon the cross, but that he might also give us in his holy Supper his body to eat and his blood to drink unto our salvation; we pray thee: give us grace to put our whole trust in thy redeeming love, and help us always so to come to this holy Sacrament that our faith in him may be strengthened, our souls comforted, and we be enabled to resist all the assaults of sin and death; through the same thy dear Son, Jesus Christ our Lord. *Amen.*

The Epistle: 1 Cor. xi. 23–32.
Or: Exod. xii. 1–13.
The Gospel: John xiii. 1–15.

Good Friday.

ALMIGHTY Father, everlasting God, who didst give thine only-begotten Son to suffer the painful death of the cross, in order that he might deliver us from the power of our enemy; grant that we may so keep this day, and so thank him for his bitter sufferings and death, that we may receive the forgiveness of our sins and redemption from everlasting death; through Jesus Christ, thy dear Son, our Lord and Saviour, who liveth and reigneth with thee in the unity of the Holy Spirit, for ever and ever. *Amen.*

The Epistle: Isa. liii.
The Gospel: The Passion history.

Easter Sunday.

ALMIGHTY God, who through the death of thy Son Jesus Christ hast overcome the power of sin and death, and by his resurrection hast restored happiness and everlasting life, that we, being delivered from the power of the devil, might live in thy kingdom; grant us grace that with our whole hearts we may believe this thy word, and continuing steadfast in our faith may evermore thank and praise thee, and may serve thee in newness of life; through the same thy Son Jesus Christ, our Lord and Saviour. *Amen.*

The Epistle: 1 Cor. v. 6–8.
The Gospel: Mar. xvi. 1–8.

Easter Monday.

O LORD Jesus Christ, who didst draw near to thy disciples on their way to Emmaus, and didst teach them from the Scriptures concerning thy resurrection; we pray thee: draw nigh to us also, and grant us thy Spirit, that by his help we may truly understand the Scriptures which are able to make us wise unto salvation, that we may come to know thee and to continue steadfast in love toward thee unto the end, and at last be made partakers of the blessed resurrection unto life everlasting; through thee, who with the Father and the Holy Spirit livest and reignest, for ever and ever. *Amen.*

The Epistle: Acts x. 34–41.
The Gospel: Luke xxiv. 13–35.

The First Sunday after Easter   *Quasimodogeniti.*

ALMIGHTY and everlasting God, who by the death and the resurrection of thy dear Son hast brought life and immortality to light, and dost now cause the gospel of peace to be declared to us; we beseech thee; so rule us by thy Holy Spirit that we may be begotten again by the power of the resurrection of Jesus Christ unto a lively hope, and to the enjoyment of thy peace which passeth all understanding; that by true faith we may overcome the world, and at all times have the witness of thy grace; through Jesus Christ, thy Son, our Lord. *Amen.*

The Epistle. 1 John v. 4–10.
The Gospel: John xx. 19–31.

The Second Sunday after Easter.   *Misericordias.*

ALMIGHTY and everlasting God, who brought again from the dead our Lord Jesus Christ, the great Shepherd of the sheep, and who by thy word and thy Spirit dost call us unto his fold, and give unto us fullness of life; we pray thee: grant us thy Holy Spirit, so that we may hear the voice of the good Shepherd and cheerfully follow him; and do thou graciously defend us, that neither Satan, the world, nor death, may pluck us out of his hand, until the day when there shall be one Shepherd and one fold; through the same thy dear Son Jesus Christ, our Lord. *Amen.*

The Epistle: 1 Pet. ii. 21–25.
The Gospel: John x. 12–16.

The Third Sunday after Easter. Jubilate.

ALMIGHTY and everlasting God, who dost suffer us to be in heaviness for a season during our earthly pilgrimage, by reason of manifold temptations, for the trial and purifying of our faith; we pray thee: so rule our hearts by thy Holy Spirit, that we, seeking our true home in heaven, may wait in faith and patience for the glorious revelation of our Lord Jesus Christ, that when he shall appear we may see him as he is, and rejoice forever with joy unspeakable; through the same thy dear Son, our Lord. *Amen.*

The Epistle: 1 Pet. ii. 11–20.
The Gospel: John xvi. 16–23.

The Fourth Sunday after Easter. Cantate.

ALMIGHTY and everlasting God, the Father of lights, from whom cometh down every good gift and every perfect gift, we give thanks to thee that thy dear Son, by his going again unto thee, secured for us the gift of the Holy Ghost; and we pray thee: give us obedient hearts, that we may not despise the reproof of thy Spirit, but being begotten again by the same to a lively faith through the word of truth, may have thy Son glorified in us, and may be transformed into his image; through the same, Jesus Christ thy Son, our Lord. *Amen.*

The Epistle: James i. 16–21.
The Gospel: John xvi. 5–15.

The Fifth Sunday after Easter. Rogate.

O LORD Jesus Christ, who hast commanded us to pray in thy name, and hast given us access to the Father with confidence, and who hast graciously promised to hear us; we pray thee: grant us grace that we may not despise this thy goodness, and bestow upon us thy Holy Spirit that he may incline our hearts to fervent prayer, that he may help our infirmities, and teach us at all times to pray for those things which are needful to our everlasting salvation, and which are well pleasing to thee, who with the Father and the Holy Spirit livest and reignest, for ever and ever. *Amen.*

The Epistle: James i. 22–27.
The Gospel: John xvi. 23–30.

Ascension-day.

ALMIGHTY God, who hast raised up thy dear Son from the lowliness of his earthly state to thy right hand in the heavens; grant that like as we do joyfully believe and this day celebrate his ascension, so we may even in this present world live in spirit in heavenly things, seeking only the things which are eternal, that we may in the end be made partakers of the ascension of thy Son Jesus Christ, our Lord. *Amen.*

The Epistle: Acts i. 1–11.
The Gospel: Mar. xvi. 14–20.

Sunday after Ascension-day. Exaudi.

ALMIGHTY and everlasting God, who hast exalted thine only-begotten Son to thy heavenly glory; we pray thee: leave us not comfortless, but send unto us thy Holy Spirit, that he may in Christ's stead comfort us under all the afflictions of this mortal life, and strengthen us to the faithful profession of the truth, and thus prepare us for the eternal glory whereunto thou hast called us; through the same thy dear Son Jesus Christ, our Lord. *Amen.*

The Epistle: 1 Pet. iv. 8–11.
The Gospel: John xv. 26—xvi. 4.

Whitsunday. Pentecost.

O LORD God, our heavenly Father, who didst on the day of Pentecost pour out thy Holy Spirit, according to thy promise, upon the Apostles and first believers, and didst fill them with his power; we beseech thee: grant that we may be led by the same Spirit into all truth, and evermore rejoice in his holy comfort, and be filled with his power; through thy dear Son Jesus Christ, our Lord and Saviour. *Amen.*

The Epistle: Acts ii. 1–13.
The Gospel: John xiv. 23–31.

Whitmonday.

MOST merciful God, our heavenly Father, we render thee most humble and hearty thanks that thou didst so love the world as to give thine only-begotten Son to die for our sins upon the cross; we beseech thee: grant us grace that we may believe and put our whole trust in him, and continue faithful to him even unto the end, so that we may not perish but have everlasting life; through Jesus Christ, thy Son, our Lord and Saviour. *Amen.*

The Epistle: Acts x. 42–48.
The Gospel: John iii. 16–21.

Trinity Sunday.

ALMIGHTY and everlasting God, who hast given unto us thy servants grace, by the confession of a true faith, to acknowledge the glory of the eternal

Trinity, and in the power of the Divine Majesty to worship the Unity; we beseech thee: that thou wouldest keep us steadfast in this faith, and evermore defend us from all adversities; who livest and reignest, one God, world without end. *Amen.*

Or:

ALMIGHTY and most merciful God, our heavenly Father, we give thanks unto thee that in the Sacrament of Holy Baptism thou didst receive us as thy children, and grant us for Christ's sake, forgiveness of sins and everlasting life; we pray thee: so rule us by thy Holy Spirit, that we may never be unmindful of our baptismal covenant, but daily renounce every evil way, and serve thee in true holiness, until we shall be received by death into thy heavenly kingdom; through Jesus Christ thy Son, who liveth and reigneth with thee and the Holy Ghost, for ever and ever. *Amen.*

The Epistle: Rom. xi. 33–36.
The Gospel: John iii. 1–15.

The First Sunday after Trinity.

ALMIGHTY and everlasting God, who in thy word hast given unto us exceeding great and precious promises, that by these we might be partakers of the divine nature, having escaped the corruption that is in the world through lust; we pray thee: grant us thy Holy Spirit, that we may be awakened by thy word out of the sleep of carnal security, and firmly believing in thy dear Son, may lay hold on the gifts of everlasting life, so that being strengthened by his might we may crucify our flesh together with the lusts thereof, and in the end be received into thy presence; through Jesus Christ, thy dear Son, our Lord. *Amen.*

The Epistle: 1 John iv. 16–21.
The Gospel: Luke xvi. 19–31.

The Second Sunday after Trinity.

MOST merciful God and Father, we render thanks unto thee, that thou didst choose us in Christ before the foundation of the world to the kingdom of thy glory, and didst call us to the same through thy word and sacrament; and we humbly pray thee: give us thy Holy Spirit, that he may purify our hearts from the vain desires of the world, that we may not despise thy heavenly calling, but obey the same with thanksgiving and joy, and continuing in fear and love toward thee, at last be made partakers of the blessed inheritance of thy children, and of the heavenly supper of the Lamb; through the same thy Son, our Lord and Saviour. *Amen.*

The Epistle: 1 John iii. 13–18.
The Gospel: Luke xiv. 16–24.

The Third Sunday after Trinity.

ALMIGHTY and everlasting God, we give thanks unto thee that in Christ Jesus our Lord thou hast manifested thy unspeakable love and mercy unto us poor sinners; and we pray thee: give us thy Holy Spirit that he may lead us to thy dear Son, and that we, believing in thy mercy, may evermore feel its power, and put our trust in thy grace alone; through Jesus Christ our Lord. *Amen.*

The Epistle: 1 Peter v. 6–11.
The Gospel: Luke xv. 1–10.

The Fourth Sunday after Trinity.

ALMIGHTY and everlasting God, by whose free grace we are what we are, and to whose unmerited mercy in Christ Jesus we owe all in us that is well-pleasing in thy sight; we pray thee: give us thy Holy Spirit, that he may write these things with power in our hearts, so that we may not with secure presumption and haughtiness judge and despise our fellow-men, but at all times, in meekness and charity, show the same forbearance towards them; through Jesus Christ our Lord. *Amen.*

The Epistle: Rom. viii. 18–23.
The Gospel: Luke vi. 36–42.

The Fifth Sunday after Trinity.

ALMIGHTY and everlasting God, who hast in mercy given us thy blessed word to teach us, that notwithstanding our sins, we may draw nigh to thee with confidence through Jesus Christ our Lord; we humbly beseech thee: give us thy Holy Spirit that we may heartily believe thy word, and be strengthened thereby to renounce the world and deny ourselves, and cheerfully to take up our cross and follow Jesus Christ, and thus be made partakers of thy everlasting glory; through the same thy Son, our Lord and Saviour. *Amen.*

The Epistle: 1 Pet. iii. 8–15
The Gospel: Luke v. 1–11.

The Sixth Sunday after Trinity.

ALMIGHTY and everlasting God, who searchest the heart and triest the reins of the children of men, with whom that faith alone availeth which worketh by love; we pray thee: beget within us an earnest desire to lay hold of thy grace in Christ, and may we be strengthened thereby to walk in the way of thy commandments; but especially do we beseech thee to cleanse our hearts by thy Holy Spirit from all malice and anger, and to fill us with that sincere love to our brethren which is well pleasing unto thee; for the sake of Jesus Christ, thy dear Son, our Lord. *Amen.*

The Epistle: Rom. vi. 3–11.
The Gospel: Mat. v. 20–26.

The Seventh Sunday after Trinity.

ALMIGHTY God, our heavenly Father, whose mercies are new unto us every morning, and who, though we have in no wise deserved thy goodness, dost abundantly provide for all our wants of body and soul; we pray thee: give us thy Holy Spirit, that we may heartily acknowledge thy merciful goodness toward us, give thanks to thee for all thy benefits, and being wholly given to thee, serve thee in true obedience; through Jesus Christ, thy dear Son, our Lord. Amen.

The Epistle: Rom. vi. 19–23.
The Gospel: Mar. viii. 1–9.

The Eighth Sunday after Trinity.

O LORD God, our heavenly Father, who in thy word hast set before us the sure way of salvation, and by the Holy Spirit dost reprove, teach, and admonish us; we beseech thee: raise up continually in thy Church faithful pastors and teachers, and graciously defend us from all error and false doctrine, that we may not be tossed and carried about by every wind of doctrine, but may try the spirits by the testimonies of thy word whether they be of thee, and cheerfully hear and obey thy servants, and finally appear before thee with the good fruits of righteousness; through Jesus Christ, thy dear Son, our Lord. Amen.

The Epistle: Rom. viii. 12–17.
The Gospel: Mat. vii. 15–23.

The Ninth Sunday after Trinity.

O LORD God, our heavenly Father, who hast appointed us to be stewards of thy gifts, and who alone canst defend and preserve us amid the temptations of this world; we pray thee: give us thy Holy

Spirit that we may use the gifts of this life which thou hast entrusted to us as faithful stewards in accordance with thy will, that when thou shalt call us to account we may be received into the habitations of the just; through Jesus Christ, thy Son, our Lord. Amen.

The Epistle: 1 Cor. x. 6–13.
The Gospel: Luke xvi. 1–9.

The Tenth Sunday after Trinity.

ALMIGHTY God, our heavenly Father, who wilt have all men to be saved, and hast no pleasure in the death of the wicked, but that the wicked turn from his way and live; we humbly beseech thee: give us thy good Spirit, that in this our time of grace we may earnestly consider the things which belong to our peace; and do thou so enlighten us that we may truly understand and forsake our sins, and thus escaping the destruction of the world, may appear before thy presence with exceeding joy; through Jesus Christ, thy dear Son, our Lord and Saviour. Amen.

The Epistle: 1 Cor. xii. 1–11.
The Gospel: Luke xix. 41–48.

The Eleventh Sunday after Trinity.

ALMIGHTY and everlasting God, who in thy holy word hast made known to us thy gracious purpose to save us by grace alone, not for any merit or worthiness in us, but solely for the sake of the precious merits of thy dear Son Jesus Christ; we pray thee: let the bright light of thy gospel shine into our hearts, that we giving up all confidence in our own righteousness, may come before thee with an humble confession of our sins, and with hearty faith put all our trust in thy grace; through Jesus Christ, thy Son, our Lord. Amen.

The Epistle: 1 Cor. xv. 1–10.
The Gospel: Luke xviii. 9–14.

The Twelfth Sunday after Trinity.

ALMIGHTY and everlasting God, who by thy mighty power dost make the blind to see, the deaf to hear, and the dumb to speak; we pray thee: take away the covering from our eyes that we may see the brightness of thy gospel, open our ears that we may diligently hear and keep thy saving word, and loosen our tongues, that with cheerful voice we may evermore praise and glorify thee; through Jesus Christ, thy dear Son, our Lord. *Amen.*

The Epistle: 2 Cor. iii. 4–11
The Gospel: Mark vii. 31–37.

The Thirteenth Sunday after Trinity.

ALMIGHTY and everlasting God, we give thee hearty thanks that it hath pleased thee to appoint our lot in the times of the new covenant, when thou desirest to make manifest thy dear Son in our hearts by faith, and to fill us with sincere love to thee and to one another; and we humbly beseech thee: grant us thy Holy Spirit, that we may learn to be duly sensible of this thine unmerited grace, and by faithfully using the same become partakers of thy salvation; for the sake of Jesus Christ, thy dear Son, our Lord. *Amen.*

The Epistle: Gal. iii. 15–22.
The Gospel: Luke x. 23–37.

The Fourteenth Sunday after Trinity.

ALMIGHTY and everlasting God, who of thy great mercy in Jesus Christ thy Son, hast granted us the forgiveness of our sins, and all things that pertain to life and godliness; we pray thee: give us thy Holy Spirit that he may so rule our hearts, that we, being ever mindful of thy fatherly love to us, may be enabled to mortify our flesh, to overcome all the lusts of the world, and serving thee in holiness and purity of life, evermore give thanks to thee for all thy goodness; through Jesus Christ, thy dear Son, our Lord. *Amen.*

The Epistle: Gal. v. 16–24.
The Gospel: Luke xvii. 11–19.

The Fifteenth Sunday after Trinity.

ALMIGHTY and most merciful God, who spared not thine only begotten Son, but freely delivered him up for us all, and thereby made manifest thine exceeding great love to us, to the end that we might be drawn to love thee again with our whole heart; we give thanks to thee for all the benefits which thou hast so richly bestowed upon us; and we humbly pray thee: give us thy good Spirit that we may not yield our hearts to the service of the world, but with filial trust serve thee alone, and seek first of all thy kingdom and its righteousness; through Jesus Christ, thy Son, our Lord. *Amen.*

The Epistle: Gal. v. 25—vi. 10.
The Gospel: Mat. vi. 24–34.

The Sixteenth Sunday after Trinity.

O LORD Jesus Christ, thou Prince of life and Conqueror of death, as by reason of our sinful nature we have all been made subject to death, and must at the last depart this life; we pray thee: grant that our hearts may have comfort in thine own glorious resurrection from the dead, and help us steadfastly to believe, that as by the word of thy power, thou didst raise from the dead the widow's son, so thou wilt also raise us up at the last day, and grant unto us everlasting life; who with the Father and the Holy Spirit livest and reignest, world without end. *Amen.*

The Epistle: Ephes. iii. 13–21.
The Gospel: Luke vii. 11–17.

The Seventeenth Sunday after Trinity.

ALMIGHTY and everlasting God, who in thy Son Jesus Christ our Saviour, hast set before us a perfect example of humility and love; we pray thee: give us thy Holy Spirit that he may teach us that only that faith availeth with thee which proceedeth from true humility of heart and which worketh by love; through Jesus Christ, thy dear Son, our Lord. Amen.

The Epistle: Ephes. iv. 1–6.
The Gospel: Luke xiv. 1–11.

The Eighteenth Sunday after Trinity.

ALMIGHTY God, our heavenly Father, who by thy word dost show unto us the way to heaven, and give us all things that pertain unto life and godliness, the knowledge both of thy holy law and of thy fatherly grace in Jesus Christ; we pray thee make the preaching of thy holy gospel powerful and effectual in us, that we may see our own sinfulness and learn to know thy dear Son as the only Saviour of sinners, in all things heartily do thy will, and with steadfast faith look for the day of our Lord Jesus Christ, to whom, with thee and the Holy Ghost, be honor and glory, for ever and ever. Amen.

The Epistle: 1 Cor. i. 4–9.
The Gospel: Mat. xxii. 34–46.

The Nineteenth Sunday after Trinity.

ALMIGHTY and everlasting God, who through Jesus Christ our Lord dost graciously pardon the sins of the contrite when they call upon thee; we pray thee: have mercy upon us and pardon all our sins, and strengthen us by thy grace that we may put off concerning our former conversation, the old man, which is corrupt according to the deceitful lusts; and being renewed in the spirit of our minds, may walk before thee in righteousness and true holiness all the days of our life; through Jesus Christ, thy dear Son, our Lord. *Amen.*

The Epistle: Ephes. iv. 22–28.
The Gospel: Mat. ix. 1–8.

The Twentieth Sunday after Trinity.

ALMIGHTY God, our heavenly Father, who in holy Baptism didst clothe us with the true wedding garment for thy blessed supper, and by thy word art continually inviting us to come to the same; we beseech thee: enlighten us by thy Holy Spirit that we may not by unbelief and lightness of mind despise thy heavenly calling, but giving heed thereto with true faith and earnestness, may walk worthy thereof in holiness of life; through Jesus Christ, thy dear Son, our Lord. *Amen.*

The Epistle: Ephes. v. 15–21.
The Gospel: Mat. xxii. 1–14.

The Twenty-first Sunday after Trinity.

O LORD Jesus Christ, who dost not break the bruised reed nor quench the smoking flax; we pray thee: increase and strengthen our imperfect faith, that we, putting our whole trust in thy word, may not only believe in thee ourselves, but strive by thy grace to bring all of our household to the like faith, that with them we may finally come to the enjoyment of everlasting life; through thee, who with the Father and the Holy Ghost livest and reignest, for ever and ever. *Amen.*

The Epistle: Ephes. vi. 10–17.
The Gospel: John iv. 47–54.

The Twenty-second Sunday after Trinity.

ALMIGHTY God, most merciful Father, who in Jesus Christ our Lord dost richly and daily forgive us all our sins, and dost graciously remit the punishment which we most justly have deserved; we pray thee: give us thy Holy Spirit, that we may so believe in thy fatherly mercy, that with a ready heart and true charity we may forgive our brethren their sins, even as thou forgivest us; through Jesus Christ our Lord. *Amen.*

The Epistle: Phil. i. 3–11.
The Gospel: Mat. xviii. 23–35.

The Twenty-third Sunday after Trinity.

ALMIGHTY and everlasting God, thou King of kings and Lord of lords, who hast appointed human government for our good; we pray thee: grant thy grace unto all Christian governments, that by exercising justice, wisdom, and mercy, they may always serve thee; and so rule us by thy good Spirit, that we may always yield a willing obedience to the laws which are ordained, and render due honor to all who are in authority, making supplication for them, that under their government and protection we may lead a quiet and peaceable life, in all godliness and honesty; through Jesus Christ our Lord. *Amen.*

The Epistle: Phil. iii. 17–21.
The Gospel: Mat. xxii. 15–22.

The Twenty-fourth Sunday after Trinity.

O GOD of all grace, from whom all our help doth come, our refuge and strength, who by thy dear Son hast promised us forgiveness of sins and deliverance from everlasting death; we pray thee: strengthen us by thy Holy Spirit, that firmly relying upon thy promises, we may daily grow in grace, and ever hold fast the comfortable hope, that we shall not see death, but fall asleep, and at the last day be raised up to everlasting life; through the same thy Son, our Lord and Saviour Jesus Christ. *Amen.*

The Epistle: Col. i. 9–14.
The Gospel: Mat. ix. 18–26.

The Twenty-fifth Sunday after Trinity.

ALMIGHTY and everlasting God, who dost not threaten in vain, but wilt surely visit the judgments of thy divine wrath upon the unbeliever and the disobedient; we give thee hearty thanks, that of thy fatherly goodness, thou hast given us warning in thy word, of all the danger and destruction that threaten our souls; and we pray thee: awaken us by thy Holy Spirit, that we may not wilfully despise thy warnings and threatenings, but may earnestly watch and pray, and by thy grace work out our salvation with fear and trembling; through Jesus Christ, thy dear Son, our Lord. *Amen.*

The Epistle: 1 Thess. iv. 13–18.
The Gospel: Mat. xxiv. 15–28.

The Twenty-Sixth Sunday after Trinity.

ALMIGHTY and everlasting God, who hast appointed thy Son Jesus Christ to be the Judge of the living and the dead, and by him wilt make manifest the counsels of all hearts; we humbly pray thee: awaken us in this our time of grace by thy Holy Spirit, that we may not live securely in our sins, but by hearty repentance and true faith lay hold on the salvation which is offered to us, and leading a godly life, look for the coming of our Lord Jesus Christ, and finally inherit the everlasting kingdom prepared for us at thy right hand, by him, who liveth and reigneth with thee and the Holy Ghost, for ever and ever. *Amen.*

·*The Epistle:* 2 Pet. iii. 3–14.
Or: 2 Thess. i. 3–10.
The Gospel: Mat. xxv. 31–46.

The Twenty-seventh Sunday after Trinity.

ALMIGHTY and everlasting God, who in the day of the glorious coming of thy dear Son, wilt deliver us from all the dangers and temptations of this mortal life, and receive us into thy heavenly kingdom; we pray thee: give us true wisdom, that while we yet have time, we may by thy grace supply ourselves with the oil of true faith, and thus prepared, always watch and pray, that when the Bridegroom cometh we may go to meet him with joy, and not be made ashamed; through Jesus Christ, thy dear Son, our Lord. *Amen.*

The Epistle: 1 Thess. v. 1–11.
Or: Rom. iii. 21–28.
The Gospel: Mat. xxv. 1–13.
Or: Mat. xxiv. 37–51.
Or: Mat. v. 1–2.

The Festival of Harvest.

ALMIGHTY God, most merciful Father, who openest thy liberal hand and satisfiest the desires of every living creature; we humbly give thanks to thee that thou hast crowned the fields with thy blessing, and hast permitted us once more to gather in the fruits of the earth; and we pray thee; bless and protect the living seed of thy word sown in our hearts, that in the plenteous fruits of righteousness, we may always present to thee an acceptable thankoffering; through Jesus Christ, thy dear Son, our Lord. *Amen.*

After a failure of the Harvest.

HOLY and merciful God, who dost rule and apportion all things in the world according to the counsel of thy will, and in thine inscrutable providence this year hast withdrawn a portion of thy blessing from our fields, and visited many of the needy with want and care, we humble ourselves before thee and acknowledge that we have deserved all thy visitations; but we also turn unto thee with steadfast faith in thy grace, and pray thee to give us patience, and to strengthen our confidence in thy help. Never leave us nor forsake us, but let us again experience thy gracious aid and blessing; for the sake of Jesus Christ, thy Son, our Lord and Saviour. *Amen.*

The Festival of the Reformation.

MOST merciful God, the Almighty protector of thy holy Church; we pray thee graciously to accept our thanks for the restoration of thy gospel; and we beseech thee evermore to defend thy Church from all error, and to preserve it in the purity of thy word; and so rule and direct our hearts by thy Holy Spirit, that we may ever continue steadfast in the faith of our Lord and Saviour, who alone is our righteousness and wisdom, our consolation and peace, and finally be brought to behold thy glory; through Jesus Christ our Lord, who liveth and reigneth with thee and the Holy Ghost, for ever and ever. *Amen.*

The Close of the Church-Year.

ALMIGHTY God, who dost rule and govern thy holy Christian Church; we give thee most hearty thanks for the plenteous blessings of thy gospel which thou hast vouchsafed unto us during the past year; and we beseech thee: bestow upon us thy Holy Spirit, that by his gracious working we may be made rightly to value thy precious means of grace, so that we, being turned to thee, may come to everlasting life; through Jesus Christ, thy dear Son, our Lord. *Amen.*

For a Day of Humiliation.

ALMIGHTY and most merciful God, our heavenly Father, who desirest not the death of a sinner, but rather that he may turn from his wickedness and live; we most earnestly beseech thee to turn from us those punishments which by our sins we most justly have deserved, and to grant us grace ever hereafter to serve thee in holiness and pureness of living; through Jesus Christ, thy dear Son, who liveth and reigneth with thee in the unity of the Holy Spirit, for ever and ever. *Amen.*

For a Day of Thanksgiving.

ALMIGHTY God, our heavenly Father, from whom all good gifts continually do proceed, and who dost daily defend us from all danger and harm; we give thee most hearty thanks for all the mercies and loving-kindness which thou hast shown unto us; they cannot be reckoned up in order unto thee, they are more than can be numbered; and we humbly beseech thee: grant us thy Holy Spirit, that we may have a due sense of all thy goodness and mercy, that we may never forget thy faithfulness and grace, but at all times give thanks unto thee, and laud and praise thy holy name, both while we live on earth, and in thine eternal kingdom. For thine, O Lord, thine only, is the kingdom, and the power, and the glory, for ever and ever. *Amen.*

General Collects.

1.

O GOD, our heavenly Father, who dost teach the hearts of thy faithful people, by sending to them the light of thy Holy Spirit; grant us by the same Spirit to have a right judgment in all things, and evermore to rejoice in his holy comfort; through the merits of Christ Jesus our Saviour, who liveth and reigneth with thee, in the unity of the same Spirit, one God, world without end. *Amen.*

2.

ALMIGHTY God, our heavenly Father, who of thy tender mercy towards us poor sinners, hast given thy only-begotten Son, that believing in him we might have everlasting life; we pray thee: grant us thy Holy Spirit that we may truly believe in him, and continuing steadfast in this faith to the end, may come to everlasting life; through Jesus Christ, thy Son, our Lord. *Amen.*

3.

ALMIGHTY and everlasting God, who through thy Son hast promised us forgiveness of sins and everlasting life; we beseech thee that thou wouldest so rule and govern our hearts by thy Holy Spirit, that in our daily need, and especially in all time of temptation, we may seek help from him, and by a true and confident faith in his word assuredly find it; through the same thy Son, our Lord Jesus Christ, who liveth and reigneth with thee and the Holy Ghost, for ever and ever. *Amen.*

4.

ALMIGHTY and most merciful God, we are now assembled in thy presence to hear all that shall be spoken in thy name and by thy command; we pray thee: grant that we may receive thy word with true devotion and faithfully keep it. Remove from us all vain and sinful thoughts, and open our hearts by thy Holy Spirit, that through the preaching of thy blessed word, we may be made truly to know thy will, and to conform our lives thereto, to the praise and glory of thy holy name, and to the salvation of our souls; through Jesus Christ our Lord and Saviour. *Amen.*

Collects for the close of the service.

1.

ALMIGHTY and everlasting God, the Father of our Lord Jesus Christ, we give thee most hearty thanks that thou hast again declared unto us thy gracious purposes of mercy toward us and toward all the children of men; and we humbly beseech thee to bless thy word which we have now heard, making it quick and powerful, and grant us grace to receive the same with sincere hearts, and to bring forth the peaceable fruits of righteousness in our lives. Do thou so rule and govern the members of thy church and the ministers of the gospel, by thy Holy Spirit, that they may ever continue steadfast in the saving doctrines of thy word, that so they may increase in faith toward thee, in charity toward all their brethren of mankind, and as becometh Christians, may show forth the excellences of him, who has called us out of darkness into his marvellous light.

And whatever other things are needful and good for us, and for which thou hast taught us to pray, we humbly ask of thee in the words of our Lord Jesus

Christ: Our Father, who art in heaven; Hallowed be thy name; Thy kingdom come; Thy will be done on earth as it is in heaven; Give us this day our daily bread; And forgive us our trespasses, as we forgive those who trespass against us; And lead us not into temptation; But deliver us from evil; For thine is the kingdom, and the power, and the glory, for ever and ever. *Amen.*

2.

O GOD, the eternal source of wisdom and purity, from whom all good counsels, all holy desires, and all just works do proceed; we offer up our prayers unto thee, beseeching thee to sanctify our hearts by thy holy word. What we know not teach thou us. Whatever is wrong in us, dispose and enable us to reform. Whatever in us is good, assist us to carry forward to perfection. Grant that we may go forth into the world with the spirit of true religion in our souls, and spend all our days in thy fear and love; that we may depart from this scene of discipline, whenever thou shalt take us away, with Christian hope, and be admitted into thy sacred temple above; through Jesus Christ our Lord. *Amen.*

3.

ALMIGHTY God, our heavenly Father, through whose infinite goodness we have been permitted to offer up our united supplications, and to meditate upon the interests of our immortal souls: hear thou in heaven, we beseech thee, the petitions of our hearts, and give thy blessing to the lessons which we have learned, as far as they agree with thy truth in scripture. Establish our minds in the love of every Christian ordinance and duty. Grant, that this house of prayer may become and continue to us the gate of heaven, the temple of devout and holy joy, the refuge of our souls from the trials and temptations of life, the school of genuine wisdom and virtue. Fit us more and more perfectly for glorifying thy name upon earth, and for singing thy praise in the mansions of thy house above; through Jesus Christ our Mediator and Redeemer. *Amen.*

4.

GRANT, we beseech thee, Almighty God, that the words, which we have heard this day with our outward ears, may be so grafted inwardly in our hearts, that they may bring forth in us the fruit of good living, to the honor and praise of thy name; through Jesus Christ our Lord. *Amen.*

Special Collects.

For the forgiveness of sins.

1.

ALMIGHTY and most merciful God, our heavenly Father, who art full of compassion and gracious, long suffering and plenteous in mercy and truth, forgiving iniquity, transgression and sin; we have sinned with our fathers, and have done perversely, we have committed wickedness, and have grievously offended thee; against thee, thee only, have we sinned, and done evil in thy sight. But, O Lord, remember not against us former iniquities; let thy tender mercies speedily prevent us; for we are brought very low. Help us, O God of our salvation, deliver us, and purge away our sins, for the glory of thy holy name, and for the sake of thy dear Son, our Saviour Jesus Christ, who liveth and reigneth with thee in the unity of the Holy Spirit, true God, world without end. *Amen.*

2.

ALMIGHTY God, our heavenly Father; we beseech thee: that thou wouldst graciously spare us, and though by our continual sins we have justly deserved thy punishment, be favorable unto us, and mercifully turn from us the punishments which we most justly have deserved; and grant, that being finally delivered from the sin, distress, and misery of this mortal life, we may be inheritors of thine everlasting righteousness and blessedness; for the sake of Jesus Christ, thy dear Son, our Lord. *Amen.*

3.

ALMIGHTY and everlasting God, who hatest nothing that thou hast made, and dost forgive the sins of all those who are penitent; create and make in us new and contrite hearts, that we worthily lamenting our sins, and acknowledging our wretchedness, may obtain of thee, the God of all mercy, perfect remission and forgiveness; through Jesus Christ our Lord. *Amen.*

For faith and a godly life.

4.

ALMIGHTY God, our heavenly Father, grant us, we beseech thee, a steadfast faith in Jesus Christ, a cheerful hope in thy mercy against all the wickedness of our sinful conscience, and a sincere love to thee and to all our fellow men; for the sake of Jesus Christ, thy dear Son, our Lord. *Amen.*

5.

GRANT to us, Lord, we beseech thee, the spirit to think and do always such things as are right;

that we, who cannot do anything that is good without thee, may by thee be enabled to live according to thy will; through Jesus Christ our Lord, who liveth and reigneth with thee and the Holy Ghost, one God, for ever and ever. *Amen.*

6.

O LORD God, our heavenly Father, who didst send thy Son, our Lord Jesus Christ into the world, that he might defend and protect us in our frailty from the power and assaults of the devil; preserve us, we beseech thee from all false security, and in all our temptations, help us, by thy Holy Spirit, to walk according to thy word, that we may never fall into the power of the adversary, but in the end be saved for ever; through the same thy Son, Jesus Christ our Lord. *Amen.*

For bodily and spiritual blessings.

7.

ALMIGHTY God, our heavenly Father, who by the word of thy power dost create and uphold all things, and from whom all the blessings of this life do come; we beseech thee: that thou wouldest make known unto us thine eternal Word, our Lord Jesus Christ, and implant him in our hearts, to the end that by thy grace we may be made worthy to receive thy divine blessing upon the fruits of the earth, and upon all that pertains to our bodily wants, and may employ all thy gifts to the praise of thy name, and the good of our fellow-men; through the same our Lord Jesus Christ, who liveth and reigneth with thee in the unity of the Holy Spirit, world without end. *Amen.*

8.

O God, the giver of all good gifts, our only help in time of need, without whose grace we can do no good thing grant to us thy humble servants, that by thy holy inspiration we may think those things that are good, and by thy merciful guiding may perform the same; through our Lord Jesus Christ. *Amen.*

9.

O GOD, the protector of all that trust in thee, without whom nothing is strong, nothing is holy; increase and multiply upon us thy mercy; that, thou being our ruler and guide, we may so pass through things temporal, that we finally lose not the things eternal; through Jesus Christ, thine only Son, our blessed Lord, who liveth and reigneth with thee and the Holy Ghost, true God, world without end. *Amen.*

For peace.

10.

ALMIGHTY and everlasting God, the King of Glory, and Lord of heaven and earth, by whose Spirit all things are governed, by whose Providence all things are ordered, who art the God of peace, and the author of all concord; forgive us, we beseech thee, our sins, and grant us thy heavenly peace and concord, that we may serve thee with fear and trembling, to the honor and glory of thy name; through Jesus Christ thy Son our Lord, who liveth and reigneth with thee in the unity of the Holy Spirit, world without end. *Amen.*

11.

O GOD, from whom all holy desires, all good counsels, and all just works do proceed; give unto thy servants that peace, which the world cannot give;

that our hearts may be set to obey thy commandments, and also that by thee, we, being defended from the fear of our enemies, may pass our time in rest and quietness; through the merits of Jesus Christ our Saviour. *Amen.*

12.

O GOD, who art the author of peace and lover of concord, in knowledge of whom standeth our eternal life, whose service is perfect freedom; defend us thy humble servants in all assaults of our enemies; that we, surely trusting in thy defence, may not fear the power of any adversaries, through the might of Jesus Christ our Lord. *Amen.*

For protection and help in affliction and distress.

13.

O LORD God, our heavenly Father, who dost see good to visit us with afflictions and trials in this present world, for our profit, but dost mercifully promise everlasting comfort and joy in the world to come to those who believe in thee; grant us thy Holy Spirit, that we may be duly sensible of this thy fatherly correction, and not despair in our tribulations, but patiently look for thy merciful help; and being always mindful of the joys of the blessed life eternal, may comfort ourselves with the same; through Jesus Christ, thy dear Son, our Lord. *Amen.*

14.

ALMIGHTY and everlasting God, the Comforter of the distressed and the Strengthener of the weak; graciously hear the prayers of all those who cry unto thee in their troubles and distress, and grant unto them help and comfort in their time of need;

through Jesus Christ thy Son, who liveth and reigneth with thee in the unity of the Holy Spirit, ever one God, world without end. *Amen.*

15.

ALMIGHTY and most merciful God, who hast appointed us to endure sufferings and death with our Lord Jesus Christ, before we enter with him into eternal glory; grant us grace at all times to subject ourselves to thy holy will, and to continue steadfast in the true faith unto the end of our lives, that so we may find comfort and joy in the blessed resurrection of the dead, and the glory of the world to come; through Jesus Christ our Lord. *Amen.*

For those who have erred.

16.

ALMIGHTY God, our heavenly Father, thy property is always to have mercy; we do therefore most earnestly beseech thee, to visit with thy fatherly correction all such as have erred and gone astray from the truth of thy holy word, and bring them to a due sense of their error; to the end that they may again with hearty faith receive and hold fast thy unchangeable and everlasting truth; through our Lord Jesus Christ thy Son, who liveth and reigneth with thee in the unity of the Holy Spirit, true God, world without end. *Amen.*

17.

ALMIGHTY God, who showest to them that are in error the light of thy truth, to the intent that they may return into the way of righteousness; grant unto all those who are named with the name of Christ, that they may avoid those things that are contrary to their profession, and follow all such things as are agreeable to the same; through our Lord Jesus Christ. *Amen.*

For favorable weather.

18.

O God, our heavenly Father, who art gracious and merciful, and who hast promised through thy Son, that thou wouldest in mercy remember us in every time of need; we beseech thee not to regard our transgressions, but our need, and thy goodness; and send us favorable weather, that by thy goodness we may receive our daily bread, and acknowledge and give thanks unto thee, most gracious God, who livest and reignest with thy Son our Lord Jesus Christ and the Holy Ghost, ever one God, world without end. *Amen.*

In time of great sickness and mortality.

19.

ALMIGHTY and most merciful God, our heavenly Father; we, thine erring children, do humbly confess unto thee that we have justly deserved the chastening, which for our sins thou hast sent upon us; but we entreat thee, that of thy boundless goodness and mercy, thou wouldest bring us to true repentance, graciously forgive our sins, and remove from us, or lighten, our deserved punishment; and grant that as obedient children we may be subject to thy will, and if it be thy pleasure, bear our afflictions in patience; through Jesus Christ our Lord. *Amen.*

For the Church.

20.

O GOD, our heavenly Father; we beseech thee to keep us continually in thy grace, to forgive us all our sins and transgressions, and mercifully to uphold us in all time of temptation; and that it would please thee, for the glory of thy most holy name, to restrain all the enemies of thy word, and to grant unto thy whole Christian Church upon the earth, grace and peace; through Jesus Christ our Lord. *Amen.*

For the Children of the Church.

21.

ALMIGHTY and everlasting God, whose will it is that not one of these little ones should perish, but who hast sent thine only Son to seek and to save that which was lost, and hast given command through the same, to suffer little children to come unto thee, and forbid them not, for of such is the kingdom of heaven; we heartily beseech thee, that thou wouldest so bless and govern the children of thy Church, by thy Holy Spirit, that they may grow in grace, and in the knowledge of thy word; and do thou protect and defend them against all danger and harm, giving thy holy angels charge over them; for the sake of Jesus Christ, thy dear Son, our Lord. *Amen.*

V.
General Prayers,
TO BE USED AT MORNING AND EVENING SERVICE.

1.

ALMIGHTY and most merciful God, we desire to lift up our hearts unto thee, the hearer of prayer, from whom alone cometh our help. Thy mercy is from everlasting to everlasting upon them that fear thee; and thy righteousness unto children's children. We, thine unworthy servants, do give thee most humble and hearty thanks for all thy goodness and loving-kindness to us, and to all men. We bless thee for our creation, preservation, and all the blessings of this life; but, above all, for thine inestimable love in the redemption of the world by our Lord and Saviour Jesus Christ, for the means of grace, and for the hope of glory. And we beseech thee to give us that due sense of all thy mercies, that our hearts may be unfeignedly thankful, and that we may show forth thy praise, not only with our lips, but in our lives. Grant, that we may devote ourselves to thy service, and walk before thee in holiness and righteousness all our days. Enable us to cherish, and to exercise habitually every pious and virtuous affection; that we may enjoy the testimony of a good conscience, and the hope of thy favor, be sustained and comforted under the troubles of this life, and finally be received into thine everlasting kingdom, through thine infinite mercy in Jesus Christ our Saviour.

Thou hast directed us, Almighty God, to offer up our supplications for all our fellow-men. We humbly beseech thee for all sorts and conditions of men; that thou wouldest be pleased to make thy ways known unto them, the saving gospel of thy Son unto all nations; that idolatry, superstition, and vice may be banished from the earth; and that war, oppression, and injustice, may forever cease. We pray that the Church of Jesus Christ throughout the world may be so guided and governed by thy good Spirit, that all who profess themselves Christians, may be led into the way of truth, and hold the faith in unity of spirit, in the bond of peace, and in righteousness of life.

We commend to thy fatherly goodness all those who are afflicted, or distressed, in mind, body, or estate; that it may please thee to comfort and relieve them, according to their several necessities; giving them patience under their sufferings, and a happy issue out of all their afflictions.

We implore thy heavenly blessing upon the land in which we live. Give success, we pray thee, to the lawful and virtuous labors of its inhabitants; and provide the necessary supplies for all their wants. Behold with thy favor the President of the United States, the Governor of this State, and all others in authority; and so replenish them with thy grace, that they may always incline to thy will, and walk in thy way, and be enabled to promote and secure the peace, liberty, and prosperity of the nation.

Send down upon all ministers of the gospel, and upon all congregations committed to their charge, the needful spirit of thy grace, that they may truly please thee; and give such efficacy to the means of education with which thou hast furnished us, that we may become a wise and righteous people, whom thou wilt delight to protect and favor.

Hear us, most merciful God, we beseech thee, in these our supplications and intercessions, which we offer up unto thee in the name of Jesus Christ thy Son our Lord. *Amen.*

2.

O GOD of all mercy, the Father of our Lord Jesus Christ, who hast promised to hear the prayer of the distressed, and not to turn away thine ear from their supplications, we thine unworthy children, come before thee to offer our petitions at the throne of thy grace. And as thou hast commanded us not only to pray for ourselves, but also to make intercessions for all men, and hast graciously promised to hear us, we would come in obedience to thy command, and humbly beseech thee to fulfill thy promise.

O Thou, who art the God and Father of all those whom thy Son has purchased with his precious blood, we beseech thee to have mercy upon all who are sitting in darkness, and upon whom the light of thy gospel has not yet shined, and to cause the knowledge of thy truth to cover the whole earth. Put an end to all superstition, and let the strongholds of unbelief be overthrown. Bless thy whole Christian Church on earth, and help all who profess the name of Christ to experience the power of the gospel unto the salvation of their souls.

And as thou hast commanded us in thy word to pray for all who are in authority, we commend to thee all the rulers of the earth; and beseech thee to grant unto them a truly Christian spirit, that the fear of the Lord may be always before their eyes, and in their hearts. Especially do we commend to thine almighty protection the land in which we live. Bestow upon the President and Congress of these United States the spirit of wisdom and of godly fear, that by their endeavors peace and concord may be established among us, to the honor of thy most holy name, and the extension of the kingdom of thy dear Son. We beseech thee, O God, to remember in mercy our State, and so to replenish with thy Spirit all whom thou hast called to exercise authority, and to administer justice, that they may love mercy and deal uprightly, and that the peaceable fruits of righteousness may every where abound among us.

We pray thee to let thy blessing rest upon this congregation, and by thy good Spirit to guide and govern its church-council, its schools, and all its labors for the advancement of thy kingdom.

Preserve peace and brotherly-love among us, and help all parents and children to be faithful to thee, and to each other.

Take under thy gracious protection the poor and the sick, the widow, and the orphan. Help all who are in need, and be merciful unto all who cry unto thee. Graciously preserve us from all national calamities, from war, scarcity, and famine, from all perils by fire and water, from pestilence and other evils which by our sins we have justly deserved. Grant unto us favorable seasons, and cause the earth abundantly to yield her increase.

O God most holy, preserve us from all sin and shame, and strengthen us by thy good Spirit that we may not forfeit thy blessing by our transgressions, nor draw down thy righteous judgment upon us. To this end enable us to make thy love our chief delight, to seek the gifts of thy Holy Spirit as our highest good, to esteem it our greatest honor to be thy children and to be like unto thee, and to prize the robes of the Redeemer's righteousness as our chief ornament. In our last hour, O God, preserve us from all the crafts and assaults of the evil one, and increase our faith in Jesus Christ, thy Son, that we may overcome all the terrors of death, and in the end inherit everlasting life, through Jesus Christ, thy dear Son, to whom, with Thee and the Holy Ghost, be honor and power, for ever and ever. *Amen.*

3.

ALMIGHTY and everlasting God, who art worthy to be had in reverence by all the children of men, we humbly give thanks unto thee for the innumerable blessings, both temporal and spiritual, which, without any merit or worthiness on our part, thou hast bestowed upon us. We praise thee especially that thou hast preserved unto us in their purity thy saving word, and the sacred ordinances of thy house.

We beseech thee, O Lord, to grant and to preserve unto thy holy church, throughout the world, purity of doctrine, and faithful pastors who shall preach thy word with power; and help all who hear rightly to understand, and truly to believe. Be thou the Protector and Defence of thy people in all times of tribulation and danger; and may we, in communion with thy holy church, and in brotherly unity with our fellow Christians, fight the good fight of faith, and in the end receive the salvation of our souls.

Bestow the influence of thy grace upon all the nations of the earth. We pray thee especially to bless our land, and all its inhabitants, and all who are in authority. Cause thy glory to dwell in our land, mercy and truth, righteousness and peace everywhere to prevail. To this end we commend to thy care all our schools and other institutions, and pray thee to make them nurseries of useful knowledge, and of Christian virtues and morals, that they may bring forth among us the wholesome fruits of life.

Graciously defend us from all calamities by fire and water, from war and pestilence, from scarcity and famine. Protect and prosper every one in his appropriate calling; and cause all useful arts to flourish among us. Be thou the God and Father of the widow and orphan, the keeper of the sick and needy, and the comforter of the forsaken and distressed.

Here special Supplications, Intercessions, and Prayers, may be offered if desired.

And as we are strangers and pilgrims on earth, having no continuing city here, help us by true faith and a godly life to prepare for the life to come; doing the work which thou hast given us to do while it is day, before the night cometh when no man can work. And when our last hour shall come, support us by thy power, and receive us into thine everlasting kingdom, through Jesus Christ, thy dear Son, our Lord, who liveth and reigneth with thee and the Holy Ghost, for ever and ever. *Amen.*

VI.
Festival Prayers,
TO BE USED AT MORNING OR EVENING SERVICE.

Advent.

1.

ALMIGHTY and everlasting God, we give thee hearty thanks, that in the fullness of the time, thou didst send unto us thine only-begotten Son, our Lord Jesus Christ; grant, we beseech thee that we may at all times be comforted by his incarnation, and truly believe that he came into the world also to save us poor sinners. O God, may he continue to come unto us through his Word and holy Sacraments, that by the help of thy grace we may so prepare our hearts, that he may take up his abode therein, and dwell in them for ever. Stir up our desires that we may look with joy for his second and last coming to judge the world, and be ready to receive him with exultation, and enter with him into the kingdom of his glory, who liveth and reigneth with thee and the Holy Spirit, for ever and ever. *Amen.*

2.

ETERNAL God, our heavenly Father, we give thanks unto thee and praise thy holy name, that thou dost this day permit us to enter in safety upon a new year in thy Church. It is of thy goodness that the light of thy holy word has been preserved among us, and that we thy people, whom thou hast redeemed with the most precious blood of thine only-begotten

Son, may even at this present time receive through thy holy Sacraments out of the fullness of thy most excellent grace spiritual strength and divine life. Glory be to thee, that according to thy mercy and faithfulness thou didst in times past cause thy holy gospel to dwell richly among us in all wisdom and understanding, and by its divine power didst reprove, correct, comfort, strengthen and support us. We would acknowledge and lament before thee, that we have brought forth in our lives so little of the fruits meet for repentance; but we beseech thee to forgive us for the sake of our Lord Jesus Christ, and to excite within us this day a renewed zeal and earnestness in the work of faith and godliness. May it please thee to bestow upon us every spiritual blessing through Jesus Christ our Lord. Endue all the ministers of thy holy word with the spirit of wisdom and of power, that utterance may be given unto them, that they may open their mouth boldly to make known the mystery of the gospel. Increase and multiply the number of those who believe and shall be saved. Awaken those who slumber in security, and raise up those who are spiritually dead. Show unto them who say, that they are rich and increased with goods and have need of nothing, their own poverty and wretchedness. Bring back those, who, having tasted the good word of God and the powers of the world to come, have turned again to the love of the world. Accomplish thy work in them in whom thy grace has begun the work of repentance and faith. Strengthen the feeble. comfort those who mourn, give the victory to those who fight the good fight of faith, preserve and defend all thy faithful servants, and prepare for a happy death all who in the counsel of thy wisdom shall depart this life before the close of this year.

O thou God of peace, sanctify us wholly. that our

spirit, and soul, and body may be preserved blameless unto the coming of our Lord Jesus Christ. Thou art faithful who hast called us and wilt also do it, to the praise of thy holy name, for the sake of our Lord Jesus Christ. *Amen.*

Christmas.

O LORD Jesus Christ, most merciful Redeemer, how shall we worthily thank thee and praise thy holy name, that of thy great mercy to us poor sinners, thou didst so deeply humble thyself as to leave thy heavenly throne, to come down to us upon the earth and to become man, even our brother, that thou mightest procure for us, peace with God, righteousness and everlasting life. O Lord how unspeakable is the love, how inconceivable the mercy wherewith thou hast loved us and brought us into union with thy heavenly Father! Thou hast begotten us again by thy holy nativity, unto thine eternal kingdom, and as by the transgression of our first parents, we were driven from thy paradise on earth, so hast thou by thy incarnation opened unto us again the door of thy paradise in heaven, that we might not remain in our misery for ever, but come to everlasting life with thee. We most heartily rejoice and give thanks to thee, that thou didst regard our low estate and raise up for us a mighty deliverance; and we most earnestly beseech thee so to enlighten our hearts that we may always rejoice in thy blessed birth, and through the power of the same overcome the dominion of sin, death, and the devil. Grant, especially, that through thy Holy Spirit, we may in all times of tribulation and sorrow comfort ourselves with thy incarnation, and in the hour of our last need may we depart this life in holy joy and peace, all which we ask, dearest Saviour for the sake of thy blessed incarnation and birth, who livest and reignest with the Father and the Holy Ghost, for ever and ever. *Amen.*

The Close of the Year.

ALMIGHTY God, our heavenly Father, we give thee hearty thanks, that in thy great goodness thou hast again preserved us during another year, and hast bestowed upon us innumerable blessings both for our bodies and souls. We humbly confess, that we have not always been duly mindful of thy goodness, but have in various ways abused thy gifts, and through our natural infirmity sinned against thee, by thought, word and deed, and have thereby most justly deserved thy wrath and indignation. But we most earnestly beseech thee to have mercy upon us, to pardon and deliver us from all our sins and wickedness. And as by thy merciful Providence, we have been brought to the close of the past, and the entrance upon a New Year, we pray thee to renew unto us thy fatherly love and faithfulness, and to grant us thy Holy Spirit, that with the year that has passed away, we may put off all our old sins, our evil desires and lusts, and with the new year begin to live a truly christian life, serving thee daily with renewed and contrite hearts. Let thy blessing be upon us, O Lord, and mercifully defend us in the coming year from all evil of body and soul. Make thy face shine upon us, and be gracious unto us; lift up thy countenance upon us, and give us thy present and everlasting peace, that we may so pass all the days of our sojourning here on earth, that after this life we may live with thee and all thy holy Angels for ever and ever, through Jesus Christ our Lord. *Amen.*

New Year.

O GOD, our heavenly Father, who hast been the refuge of thy children in all generations, and from everlasting to everlasting art the same, unchangeable in power, wisdom and goodness; another portion of our earthly pilgrimage has passed away, and in thy name we this day enter upon a New Year.

Thou, O God, art the author of our being, and the giver and preserver of all our bodily and spiritual blessings. It is thy might by which we have been sustained; it is of thy mercy that we are not consumed. Thy compassions fail not, they are new every morning, great is thy faithfulness. Year after year thou hast spared and blessed us, not dealing with us after our sins, nor rewarding us according to our iniquities. Thou hast continued to us thy holy word, the preaching of thy gospel and the right use of thy sacraments; thou hast daily supplied all our wants; thou hast filled our hearts with food and gladness and hast preserved us from plague, pestilence and other calamities, and kept and guarded us from manifold dangers. Many, O Lord, are the wonderful works which thou hast done and thy thoughts which are to us-ward; they cannot be reckoned up in order unto thee: if we would declare and speak of them they are more than can be numbered. Thou hast at times chastened us on account of our sins, but hast not removed thy loving kindness from us. For this we praise and give thanks unto thy holy name, and humbly beseech thee not to impute to us the sins which we have committed in times past, and by which we have most justly deserved thy wrath and indignation. O be merciful to us poor sinners, cease not, we pray thee to spare, to forgive, and to bless us. Suffer us not to carry one of our old sins with us into the new year unlamented, unforgiven, and unforsaken, but help us by thy grace to put on the new man, which after God is created in righteousness and holiness. Renew a right spirit within us, and let thy fatherly love and faithfulness follow us all the days of our life. Grant unto us all holy desires and just works. Take from us all sorrow, preserve us from all sin and danger, and lead us in the way everlasting.

Most merciful Father, show thy love unto all for whom it is our duty to pray. Have mercy upon all men. Preserve unto us thy word and the sacred ordinances of thy house. Enlighten, sanctify, and bless all the ministers of thy holy gospel. Build up our churches and schools. Defend us from all false doctrine and heresy. Protect our country in its important interests and direct our rulers and magistrates. Bless all parents in the discharge of their sacred obligations and incline the hearts of our children to serve thee in sincerity and truth. Save us from the calamities of war and bloodshed, from pestilence and famine. Give us fruitful seasons, that the earth may yield her increase. Prosper the work of our hands. Supply the wants of thy faithful ministers. Convert the sinner from the error of his ways, encourage and strengthen thy believers. Bring back those who have erred and gone astray. Turn the hearts of our enemies, persecutors and slanderers, and bring to nought all the designs of evil men. Protect the widow and the orphan. Provide for the poor and the destitute. Feed the hungry. Cheer the hearts of the exiled. Set free all who are innocently imprisoned. Comfort the sorrowful and the distressed. Raise up those who have been wrongfully put down. Preserve all women in the perils of child-birth, and all young children. Protect all who travel by land or water and support the souls of the dying.

And unto thee who art able to do exceedingly above all that we ask or think, be glory by Christ Jesus throughout all ages. *Amen.*

Epiphany.

ALMIGHTY and everlasting God, the merciful Father of Lights, from whom cometh down every good gift and every perfect gift, we praise and give thanks to thee, that thou didst manifest unto the wise men the new-born King of the Jews, thine only begotten Son our Lord Jesus Christ, as the blessed light of the gentiles, and in thy great mercy didst through him call us also from the darkness and shadow of death to thy marvellous light. We pray thee, so to let this blessed light always shine upon us, and so to bestow upon us the gracious enlightenment of thy Holy Spirit, that we may daily increase in the knowledge of our new-born King, honor, confess, and worship him; and taking up our cross and following him, may always walk in his light as becometh the children of light, that when our last hour shall come, we may pass with joy and comfort through the dark valley of death, and live with thee for ever in the light and glory of eternal life, through the same, thy dear Son, our Lord and Saviour Jesus Christ. *Amen.*

The Passion of Christ, or Good Friday.

1.

O LORD Jesus Christ, who by thy holy and innocent sufferings didst procure for us poor and condemnable sinners the grace of thy heavenly Father, and didst bring back to us everlasting life, we most heartily thank thee for thy sufferings and death, and the great love which thou didst thereby shew unto us. Preserve us, we beseech thee, in thine everlasting love for the sake of thy sufferings and death, and give us the grace of thy Holy Spirit, that we may with truly grateful hearts acknowledge, praise, and magnify the benefits of thy redemption, and be thereby strengthened in our faith, cheered in our hope, inspired with sincere love to thee, encouraged to be patient in all our trials and distresses, and to persevere in our obedience to thy good and gracious will, that we may be dead indeed unto sin and live unto thee, and serve thee in righteousness and true holiness all the days of our lives, and finally, depart this life in peace, and inherit everlasting life, through the merits of thy bitter sufferings and death, who livest and reignest with the Father and the Holy Ghost, for ever and ever. *Amen.*

2.

O LORD, our heavenly Father, almighty and everlasting God, who of thy great mercy to a sinful world didst not spare thine only-begotten Son, but delivered him up for us all, that through him we might be restored to everlasting life and happiness; we give thee most hearty thanks for this thy marvellous grace, in that thou hast made him to be sin for us who knew no sin; that we might be made the righteousness of God in him.

O Lord Jesus Christ, most blessed Redeemer, thou wast despised and rejected of men, a man of sorrows and acquainted with grief. The Lord hath laid on thee the iniquity of us all; thou didst surely bear our griefs and carry our sorrows; thou wast wounded for our transgressions and bruised for our iniquities; the chastisement of our peace was upon thee; and with thy stripes we are healed. Wherefore we give thee everlasting praise, that for our benefit thou didst endure all these unspeakable sufferings and wast obedient unto death, even the death of the cross. Have mercy upon us, O Lord, and save us, that not any of us may perish. As thou hast made thy soul an offering for sin, give us, we pray thee thy Holy Spirit to aid us in turning to thee; and as thou hast borne our iniquities, do thou also justify us by thy knowledge. We have made thee to serve with our sins, we have wearied thee with our iniquities; help us now, O Lord, that we may not die in our sins without true repentance, nor by our sinful life crucify thee afresh, and by our impious contempt tread under foot thy blood, which cleanseth us from our sins. Grant especially, we beseech thee, that we may with truly contrite hearts daily and earnestly contemplate thy sufferings and death, by a living faith in thee take our refuge to thy wounds, and through the merits of the same become partakers of everlasting life. Finally we pray thee to grant us grace at all times to take up our cross and to follow thee, to the end that suffering with thee, we may also be glorified together with thee in thy heavenly kingdom, where thou livest and reignest with the Father and the Holy Ghost, one God, for ever and ever. *Amen.*

Easter.

1.

GLORY and honor be unto thee, O Lord, our God, who art, and wast, and shalt be from everlasting to everlasting. Adoration and praise be unto thee, the God of our Lord Jesus Christ, the Father of glory, who hath made this day for us that we might rejoice and be glad in it. Adoration and praise be unto thee, that thy beloved Son was manifested in the flesh, that he might take away sin by the willing sacrifice of himself on the cross, bring life and immortality to light, and open the kingdom of heaven to all who believe in his name. Adoration and praise be unto thee, who art so wonderful in counsel and excellent in working. Thou hast not left his soul in hell, neither suffered thy Holy One to see corruption. Thou hast made known to him the ways of life, that through sufferings he should enter into his glory. Thou hast loosed for him the pains of death, and made him full of joy with thy countenance. Glory be to thee, that by the resurrection of Jesus his innocence is vindicated, his claims approved; that instead of the crown of thorns, he now wears a crown of glory; that he reigns for ever at thy right hand; that he is appointed to lead his followers unto living fountains of water; and that where he is, they shall be with him in blessedness everlasting.

Most merciful God, forgive we beseech thee the errors and transgressions by which we have made ourselves unworthy of such unspeakable condescension and mercy. Enlighten the eyes of our understanding, that we may know what is the hope of our calling, and help our infirmities that we may rejoice with our whole heart in his glorious gospel. Whilst we praise thee that Jesus was delivered for our offences and raised again for our justification, O quicken us together with him, that we may walk in newness of life; dead indeed unto sin, but alive unto thee. Whilst we rejoice in that lively hope to which thou hast begotten us again according to thine abundant mercy by the resurrection of Jesus Christ from the dead, the hope of an inheritance incorruptible, undefiled, and that fadeth not away,—may we purify ourselves even as he is pure, seek those things which are above, and lay up treasures in heaven. Amidst the temptations and discouragements we shall experience, may we be steadfast and immovable, always abounding in the work of the Lord; forasmuch as we know, that our labor is not in vain in the Lord. Whatever comforts thou shalt send us, may they be heightened by the reflection, that they are a foretaste of yet greater and more enduring joys. In all the afflictions of life, and in the decay of nature, may we be enabled to realize with humble and holy confidence, that our Redeemer liveth. When we are called to mourn over the loss of dear and valued friends, may we be cheered by the thought, that those who sleep in Jesus, will God bring with him. And when we ourselves shall depart this life, may we be enabled to say; O death where is thy sting? O grave where is thy victory? Thanks be to God, who giveth us the victory through our Lord Jesus Christ.

[O God, who by thy mighty power, didst overthrow the powers of darkness, and for the sufferings of death hast crowned the Captain of our salvation with glory and honor; give him, we pray thee, the heathen for his inheritance, and the uttermost parts of the earth for his possession. May all his enemies be put under his feet, and all ungodliness and wickedness be subdued. As thou hast appointed a day in which thou wilt judge the world in righteousness, and hast given assurance of it unto all men, in that thou hast raised Christ Jesus from the dead: may all in every land prepare themselves for their final account, and be made meet for an entrance into his heavenly kingdom.]

O God of all peace and comfort, have mercy upon all who are undergoing the changes and trials of this fleeting world; upon all who are oppressed by lawless might; upon all who are suffering for truth and conscience sake; upon all who are beset with temptations to sin; upon all who are sinking under the weight of disease; upon all who are ready to despair of thy grace; upon all who are tormented by the fear of death; upon all who are entering into the valley of the shadow of death. May Christ be in them the hope of glory. And at his appearing may the trial of their faith be found unto praise and honor.

Now unto thee who art able to keep us from falling, and to present us faultless before the presence of his glory with exceeding joy; to the only wise God our Saviour be glory and majesty, dominion and power, both now and ever. *Amen.*

Ascension-day.

O LORD Jesus Christ, eternal Son of God, Saviour of the world, the King of heaven and of earth, the mighty Conqueror of all our enemies, when thou hadst by thy sufferings and death accomplished the great work of redemption, thou didst arise from the dead, shew thyself alive to thy disciples, give them commandment and bless them, and then ascend up into heaven; thou hast led captivity captive, and given gifts unto men; thou hast spoiled principalities and powers and made a show of them openly, triumphing over them by thy cross. All power is given unto thee in heaven and in earth. Thou art seated at the right hand of thine everlasting Father, and art exalted above every name that is named, not only in this world, but also in that which is to come. All things are put under thy feet, and thou art the head over all things to the church. The hand writing of ordinances that was against us has been blotted out, the sentence of condemnation removed, all our guilt cancelled with thy precious blood, and our enemies, death and the devil, have now no more dominion over us. For this thy glorious and mighty victory, we render unto thee most hearty thanks; we praise thee, we worship thee, and humbly beseech thee as our everlasting High Priest to intercede for us poor sinners with thy heavenly Father, that we, being delivered from all guilt and pain through the merits of thy sufferings and death, may escape the just wrath of God and the punishment of the world to come.

We are also the children of thy heavenly Father, for thou hast said; I ascend unto my Father and your Father, and to my God and your God. Give unto us thy Holy Spirit, the Spirit of truth, the blessed Comforter, to teach, to lead, to comfort and to strengthen us, that we may evermore hold fast thy saving word, and not be carried about with every wind of doctrine by the sleight of men, and cunning craftiness, whereby they lie in wait to deceive.

And as thou, O blessed Lord, art not far off, but always nigh unto us, ruling over us as our everlasting heavenly King, we most heartily pray thee to protect, with thine almighty hand thy people whom thou hast so gloriously redeemed, as thy heritage, from Satan and all our enemies. Leave us not comfortless, but abide with us even unto the end of the world, and graciously continue unto us thy word and the right use of thy holy Sacraments; send forth faithful laborers into thy harvest, endue all thy ministers with the power of thy Holy Spirit and bless their labors, to the end that sinners may be converted unto thee, and many souls gathered into thine everlasting kingdom. O Lord Jesus Christ, Son of the Highest, by the offering up of thy body and blood, thou hast given us a sure pledge, that after this life we also shall come to the joy and felicity of everlasting life; grant that we may be encouraged by thy triumphant ascension to turn away our hearts and eyes from the perishable things of this world, and to seek those things which are above. Give us the wings of the morning that we may flee unto thee. When shall we be permitted to see thy face, and to ascend with thee to thy Father and to our Father, to thy God and to our God? May thy good Spirit, the pledge and seal of our inheritance cry within us; Come, Lord Jesus. Come quickly, Lord Jesus our Comforter. Hear our prayers and receive us, Saviour to thee. *Amen.*

Whitsunday.

1.

ALMIGHTY and everlasting God, the Father of our Lord Jesus Christ, we give thee most hearty thanks, that on this holy day of Pentecost thou didst reveal thyself from heaven, and visibly pour out the Holy Spirit upon thine Apostles in Jerusalem, and dost thereby make known, that through the power and operation of the Holy Spirit by the preaching of the Apostles and all true ministers of thy word, thou desirest to gather unto thyself from among the sinful, condemned, and lost race of man, a holy and everlasting Church, and to enlighten, sanctify and save our souls, and so to rule them by thy Holy Spirit, that we may know, honor, and worship thee as the only true God. We beseech thee most merciful Father, through Jesus Christ, our only Saviour, that it may please thee even as of old, so now also and ever hereafter to pour out thy Holy Spirit into our hearts, to purify and renew them, and to make us steadfast and immovable in our faith. O cast us not away from thy presence, and take not thy Holy Spirit from us. Restore unto us the joy of thy salvation; and uphold us with thy free Spirit, that by the word of thy truth we may be preserved in the saving faith. Bring to nought, we pray thee the wicked designs of all false teachers and ungodly men, who would lead us away from the good pasture of thy word into the destructive ways of human reason and of Satan.

May it please thee to govern with thy good Spirit the hearts of all christian Rulers. Bless the land in which we live. Enlighten and direct the President of the United States and all others in authority. Grant them in health and prosperity long to live, and enable them to secure to all our people peace, liberty, and happiness. Rule and direct by the Spirit of thy grace the hearts of all parents, children, and servants, that they may have thee always before their eyes, and fulfill the duties of their several stations in righteousness and true holiness as shall be well pleasing to thee, serving thee all the days of their lives. And do thou help us all by thy Holy Spirit, to increase in all knowledge, faith, charity, purity, and truth, and at last to receive the end of our faith, even the salvation of our souls, through our Lord Jesus Christ, who liveth and reigneth with thee and the Holy Ghost, for ever and ever. *Amen.*

2.

O LORD Jesus Christ, eternal Son of the Father, who according to thy word and promise didst send down the Holy Spirit into the hearts of thy chosen disciples, that they might go into all the world and preach the gospel to every creature; we most earnestly beseech thee to bestow upon us also the gift of thy Holy Spirit, that we may be enlightened with the true knowledge of God and purified from all uncleanness to do thy will; that so we may be made the temples and habitations of the Holy Ghost.

O God, the Holy Spirit, our only Comforter, implant within us a true faith, a joyful hope, and an ardent love to thee, and leave us not in our last hour, but cheer and support us all in our earthly trials and afflictions, and bring us to our blessed and eternal home in heaven, who livest and reignest with the Father and the Son, blessed for evermore. *Amen.*

Trinity Sunday.

ALMIGHTY, eternal, and most merciful God, the Father of our Lord and Saviour Jesus Christ, who together with the Son and the Holy Ghost didst create and dost preserve the heavens and the earth, angels and men, and all things that exist, and who of thine infinite goodness and mercy, didst by thy holy word reveal thyself to the children of men, as one eternal God, in three persons, co-equal in majesty, power, and glory. O God the Father, Son, and Holy Ghost, Most Holy and ever blessed Trinity, we worship thee in true faith, we praise thee, we acknowledge thee, we glorify thee, we give thanks to thee now and evermore, and by our prayer and pure confession, we would separate ourselves from all who do not acknowledge and worship thee as the only true and living God, but make unto themselves Gods by their own imagination, and dishonor and blaspheme thy holy name.

O God, the Father everlasting, who from all eternity didst beget a Son, and through him didst make known to us the counsel of our salvation, and hast ordained him to be the Mediator and Redeemer of the whole human race; we come before thee with humble hearts, beseeching thee to have mercy upon us, and to forgive us all our sins. O Lord God of Hosts, lift upon us the light of thy countenance, and we shall be healed. May it please thee, O Lord, to gather together a holy Church in all the parts of the world to worship and praise thy holy name, and

TRINITY SUNDAY.

to preserve unto thyself among us also a holy seed. We commend to the care of thy merciful Providence in these last evil days, the President of these United States and all others in authority, beseeching thee to grant, that by the effectual working of thy Holy Spirit, they may so rule and govern, that we may lead a quiet and peaceable life in all godliness and honesty.

O God, the everlasting Son, who art the express image of thy heavenly Father, and the brightness of his glory, who of thine unspeakable love didst take upon thee our nature, and didst make an atonement for all our sins, we praise and magnify thee for all thy goodness and mercy, and humbly acknowledge, that we can never worthily thank thee therefor. Have mercy upon us, O Lord, and cleanse us from all our sins, with thy most precious blood. Preserve to us thy holy Word, and the right use of the blessed Sacraments. Defend us from all error and false doctrine. Bring to naught the devices of all the enemies of thy word, who trouble us, that they may have no power over us to lead us in the paths of sin and destruction. Grant protection and deliverance to thy whole christian Church on earth; give to all its members steadfastness of faith, patience and comfort in all their trials and distresses, and conduct us in safety through this vale of sorrow into the kingdom of thy glory.

O God, the Holy Ghost, who art sent from the Father and the Son into our hearts to renew them; enlighten us and enkindle within us a true and saving faith. Direct and lead us into thy truth, and keep us steadfast in the same amidst all the assaults and temptations of the world, even unto the end.

O most merciful and ever-faithful God, Father, Son and Holy Ghost, most Holy and ever-blessed Trinity, grant us thy heavenly grace to persevere in the true

Christian faith, to live a godly life and to die a happy death, that after the trials and afflictions of this mortal life, we way enter into the company and fellowship of the holy angels and of the redeemed and see thee face to face, and love and praise and magnify and worship thee, world without end. *Amen.*

The Festival of Harvest.

ALMIGHTY and most merciful Father, the giver of all good and perfect gifts, we render to thee most hearty thanks, and praise thy holy name, that in these last days thou hast so richly blessed us with thy good word and the holy sacraments, and also abundantly supplied all our daily bodily wants. In thy merciful Providence thou hast again bestowed upon us a plentiful harvest of the fruits of the earth. Thou hast watered the hills from thy chambers; thou hast given us rain and sunshine in their season, and hast protected our fields from the storm and the tempest. We acknowledge and confess before thee, O God, that we are not worthy of the least of all thy benefits, that by our disobedience, ingratitude, and abuse of thy gifts, and by other manifold sins which we have committed against thee, we have most justly deserved that thou shouldst withdraw from us thy merciful visitations. But we are heartily sorry for all our ingratitude, and do earnestly repent of all our wickedness and sins. And as unto thee, O Lord, belong mercies and forgivenesses, we beseech thee in the name of our Lord Jesus Christ, deal with us, not according to our unworthiness, but according to our great need. Take not away from us thy holy word, the spiritual manna and bread of our souls. Mercifully preserve us and our children from all error and false doctrine, for thy testimonies, O Lord, are sure.

Holiness becometh thy house forever. And as thou, O God, hast permitted us again to gather in the fruits of the earth, we praise thee, we bless thee, we worship thee, we glorify thee, we give thanks to thee in the name of our Lord Jesus Christ, and humbly pray thee to sanctify all thy gifts to our use, and to incline our hearts always to do good and to distribute to the relief of the needy. Preserve us, O Lord, and continually give us those things which are necessary, as well for the body as the soul, until, in the general harvest of the world we shall be gathered into thy kingdom, and eat and drink with all thy saints in everlasting life, through Jesus Christ, thy dear Son, our Lord. *Amen.*

The Festival of the Reformation.

LORD God, our heavenly Father, from whom cometh our help and salvation! Thou didst come to the help of our fathers; thou didst deliver them from depths of misery; thou didst visit them with thy salvation. We would remember the mighty deeds which thou hast wrought, and declare thy glory from generation to generation. We therefore come before thy face this day with praise and thanksgiving.

O God, our Father in Christ Jesus our Lord, thou hast manifested thy power and faithfulness and glorified thy name; thou hast delivered the church of thy dear Son from the power of darkness; thou hast broken the degrading chains of her bondage; thou hast opened anew thy word of life unto the flock of Christ and gathered together all who thirsted after righteousness under the banner of the true and saving faith. Lord, it was thy work, and not the work of man. Thou didst raise up those faithful servants who clearly saw, and deeply felt the errors and corruptions of the church. Thou didst enlighten them with the knowledge of thy truth and set them free, that they might bring others to the blessed liberty of Christ Jesus. Thou didst inspire them with courage to stand forth in thy strength, as witnesses for thee, to assail the corruptions which had been brought into thy sanctuary, and not to fear the enmity of the mighty of this world. Humbly feeling that in their own strength they could accomplish naught, and would soon be overcome, they put their trust in thee as their tower of defence, their trusty shield and weapon. And thou didst not suffer them to be put to shame, thou didst give them the victory over thy enemies, and didst crown their work with thy blessing. Therefore we will sing of the mercies of the Lord forever; with our mouth will we make known thy faithfulness to all generations.

Thanks be to thee, O Lord, that thou hast ever since preserved unto thy church the dearly purchased heritage, that we have thy holy word without any human additions, in its purity and its power, and that the holy sacraments instituted by Christ are rightly administered among us. Thanks be to thee, that we are permitted to worship the Father in spirit and in truth, unrestrained by human laws and unmolested by worldly might; that we see the way to thee and to thy mercy-seat, open unto all through the blood of our only Mediator and Redeemer; and that we know, that there is now no need of any other sacrifice or merit, any other expiation or atonement, in order to obtain peace with thee, but only of a living faith in that redemption which is in Christ Jesus.

Most merciful God, preserve unto us evermore this invaluable blessing, that all generations to come may rejoice in it. Be thou continually the Defender, the Protector, and the Saviour of thy church. Enlighten, sanctify and bless her through thy holy word and sacraments. Grant her grace rightly to value the privileges which thou hast bestowed upon her, that she may hold fast what she hath, that no man may take her crown. Purify her from all offences, and graciously defend her from all schisms and divisions. Vouchsafe at all times to our congregations pious and faithful pastors, who shall preach thy word in its purity, constrained by the deep convictions of the heart, and accompany their preaching with the mighty influence of thy Spirit, that it may bring forth blessed fruit in the hearts and lives of Christians. Grant, O Lord, that we may dwell in thy regenerated church as thy regenerated children, walking worthily of the blessed gospel, and adorning its pure doctrine by a holy life. Help us to stand fast in the liberty wherewith Christ hath make us free, and never suffer us to become the slaves of men or of sin. Holiness becometh thine house, O Lord, forever, and to thy glory may the light of truth burn brightly upon the candlestick of every congregation. Have mercy, O God, upon all men! Bestow the blessings for which we praise thee, upon all our brethren who are still destitute of them. Restrain every where, the kingdom of darkness upon earth, and cause the light of thy truth to shine in all the world. Turn the hearts of those who hate thy word, and forgive them, because they know not what they do. Visit with thy saving power all who suffer tribulation, oppression, and persecution for conscience sake, and deliver them by thy mighty arm out of all their troubles. Enlighten and lead back those who have erred and strayed from thee, convince the doubting, strengthen the weakhearted, and make all thy children meet for their eternal and blissful inheritance in heaven. May it please thee, to bless us and all men, in Christ

Jesus our Lord, with knowledge and wisdom, with faith and love, with peace in life, and with hope in death. Lead us and all men, we beseech thee, through the darkness of time, into the light of eternity, and there present us faultless before the presence of thy glory with exceeding joy.

Now unto thee, the Father, the Son, and the Holy Ghost, be glory in the church by Christ Jesus, throughout all ages, world without end. *Amen.*

Day of Humiliation and Prayer.

ALMIGHTY, eternal, and most merciful God, Father of our Lord Jesus Christ, who, together with the Son and the Holy Ghost livest and reignest from everlasting to everlasting, and who hast created the heavens and the earth; thou hast said: Why will ye die in your sins, for I am merciful and will not keep anger forever, only acknowledge thine iniquity, that thou hast transgressed against the Lord thy God. Trusting in this merciful assurance of thy word, we poor miserable sinners come before thy divine Majesty, and confess and bewail the sins which we have committed against thee. Thou, O Lord, art holy, but we are unholy; thou art righteous, but we are unrighteous, our sins are more than can be numbered; we have ofttimes despised thy holy commandments; we have not obeyed the voice of thy beloved Son; we have resisted the call of thy Holy Spirit; we have offended our neighbor; we have brought disgrace upon thy holy gospel and sacraments, and we have abused thy gifts. O Lord, we are not worthy to be called thy children; we have rendered ourselves deserving of the punishments due to the guilty; we would not murmur against thy divine majesty, but we would humble ourselves under thy mighty hand and acknowledge thy justice. Have mercy upon us, we beseech thee, even as thou hast shown mercy unto every distressed and penitent soul from the foundation of the world. Our fathers trusted in thee: they trusted and thou didst deliver them; they cried unto thee and were delivered. Most merciful God, look upon us with the eye of compassion, for thou art our Shepherd, and we are the sheep of thy fold; thou art our Father, and we are thy children. Thy dear Son, Jesus Christ, hath borne our iniquities and carried our sorrows. Have mercy upon us, O Lord of Hosts, for the sake of the bitter sufferings and death of thy dear Son. Grant us true repentance, and thy grace always to live a godly life, and increase and strengthen our feeble faith, that we may not be hearers only, but doers of thy word and the temples of the Holy Ghost forever. Shine into our hearts with thy divine light, that in these last evil days we may have a cheerful spirit and be filled with heavenly joy. Suffer us not like the children of this world to fall into self-security and to become careless of the salvation of our souls, but incline our hearts to watch and to pray. Defend us and our children from disease, pestilence and all other evils of body and soul. Bring to naught the wicked designs of ungodly men, who dishonor and blaspheme thy holy name, and grant us thy peace. Protect and bless our government and graciously deliver our beloved country from every evil which we feel or fear. Bless thy whole Christian church on earth. And whenever it shall please thee to call us out of this vale of sorrow, may thy grace preserve us, and the Comforter, the Holy Ghost cheer and support us in our last hour, and conduct us to the joys of everlasting life, where with angels and archangels, we shall praise and give thanks to thee the Father, and the Son, and the Holy Ghost, world without end. Amen.

VII.

The Passion Services.

To be held during Passion-week, or during the Lenten season. They present the history of the Passion of our Lord as it is written by the four Evangelists. The form for opening and closing the first service is to be used at each service.

First Service.

LO, I come: in the volume of the book it is written of me, I delight to do thy will, O my God: yea, thy law is within my heart.—Ps. xl. 7, 8. I will ransom them from the power of the grave; I will redeem them from death.—Hosea xiii. 14.

Or: Psalm cxxx.

The Congregation kneeling shall devoutly pray.

O CHRIST, thou Lamb of God, that takest away the sins of the world, have mercy upon us!

O Christ, thou Lamb of God, that takest away the sins of the world, have mercy upon us!

O Christ, thou Lamb of God, that takest away the sins of the world, grant us thy peace!

OUR Father, who art in heaven; Hallowed be thy name; Thy kingdom come; Thy will be done on earth, as it is in heaven; Give us this day our daily bread; And forgive us our trespasses, as we forgive those who trespass against us; And lead us not into temptation; But deliver us from evil; For thine is the kingdom, and the power, and the glory, for ever and ever. Amen.

Then shall be sung a hymn concerning the Passion of Christ; after which the Minister shall say:

GLORY be to the Father, and to the Son, and to the Holy Ghost; as it was in the beginning, is now, and ever shall be, world without end. *Amen.*

Grace be unto you, and peace, from God our Father, and from the Lord Jesus Christ. *Amen.*

Let us pray.

MOST merciful God, the Father of our Lord Jesus Christ, we render unto thee most hearty thanks, that thou dost permit us again to draw nigh to that holy season, in which the sufferings and death upon the cross of thy beloved Son are declared unto thy Church, for the everlasting comfort of our souls.—O Lord Jesus, who hast loved us even unto death, grant unto us serious and devout hearts, that the remembrance of thy saving love, and of thy precious sufferings and death, may be sanctified unto us. We beseech thee so to strengthen us by thy grace, during this blessed season, that we may come to true repentance and the renewing of our mind in thy holy image, and that we may experience the rich comforts of true faith, love unfeigned, and the assured hope of everlasting life.— Holy Father, who wast in Christ reconciling the world unto thyself, fill us with an anxious desire, to seek and to find in thy dear Son, our crucified Redeemer, and in him alone, that salvation which he only can grant, now and forever. *Amen.*

LET us look unto Jesus, the author and finisher of our faith; who, for the joy that was set before him, endured the cross, despising the shame.—Heb. xii. 2. He humbled himself, and became obedient unto death, even the death of the cross. Wherefore God also hath highly exalted him, and given him a name which is above every name: that at the name of Jesus every knee should bow, of things in heaven, and things in earth, and things under the earth; and that every tongue should confess that Jesus Christ is Lord, to the glory of God the Father.—Phil. ii. 8–11.

HEAR to-day the first part of the history of the Passion of our Lord, as it is written by the four Evangelists. It contains the account of the council of his enemies, and his conversation with his disciples concerning his approaching sufferings, the supper at Bethany and the anointing, the entry into Jerusalem and the purifying of the temple. It reads thus:

JOHN xi. 47–53.—Then gathered the chief priests and the Pharisees a council, and said, What do we? for this man doeth many miracles. If we let him thus alone, all men will believe on him; and the Romans shall come, and take away both our place and nation. And one of them, named Caiaphas, being the high priest that same year, said unto them, Ye know nothing at all, nor consider that it is expedient for us, that one man should die for the people, and that the whole nation perish not. And this spake he not of himself: but being high priest that year, he prophesied that Jesus should die for that nation; and not for that nation only, but that also he should gather together in one the children of God that were scattered abroad. Then from that day forth they took counsel together for to put him to death.

MAT. xx. 17.—And Jesus going up to Jerusalem, took the twelve disciples apart in the way, and said unto them. LUKE xviii. 31–34.—Behold, we go up to Jerusalem, and all things that are written by the prophets concerning the Son of man shall be accomplished. For he shall be delivered unto the Gentiles, and shall be mocked, and spitefully entreated, and spitted on; and they shall scourge him, and put him to death: and the third day he shall rise again. And they understood none of these things: and this saying was hid from them, neither knew they the things which were spoken.

JOHN xii. 1, 2.—Then Jesus six days before the passover came to Bethany, where Lazarus was which had been dead, whom he raised from the dead. There they made him a supper, (MAT. xxvi. 6,) in the house of Simon the leper, (JOHN xii. 2,) and Martha served: but Lazarus was one of them that sat at the table with him. MARK xiv. 3.—As he sat at meat, there came a woman having an alabaster box of ointment of spikenard very precious; and she brake the box, and poured it on his head, (JOHN xii. 3–6,) and anointed the feet of Jesus, and wiped his feet with her hair: and the house was filled with the odor of the ointment. Then saith one of his disciples, Judas Iscariot, Simon's son, which should betray him, why was not this ointment sold for three hundred pence, and given to the poor? This he said, not that he cared for the poor; but because he was a thief, and had the bag, and bare what was put therein. MARK xiv. 4, 6–9.—And there were some that had indignation within themselves, and said, Why was this waste of the ointment made? And Jesus said, Let her alone; why trouble ye her? she hath wrought a good work on me. For ye have the poor with you always, and whensoever ye will ye may do them good: but me ye have not always. She hath done what she could: she is come aforehand to anoint my body to the burying. Verily I say unto you, Wheresoever this gospel shall be preached throughout the whole world, this also that she hath done shall be spoken of for a memorial of her.

JOHN xii. 12.—On the next day, (MAT. xxi. 1–7,) when they drew nigh unto Jerusalem, and were come to Bethphage, unto the mount of Olives, then sent

Jesus two disciples, saying unto them, Go into the village over against you, and straightway ye shall find an ass tied, and a colt with her: loose them, and bring them unto me. And if any man say aught unto you, ye shall say, The Lord hath need of them; and straightway he will send them. All this was done, that it might be fulfilled which was spoken by the prophet, saying, tell ye the daughter of Zion, Behold, thy King cometh unto thee, meek, and sitting upon an ass, and a colt the foal of an ass. And the disciples went, and did as Jesus commanded them, and brought the ass, and the colt, and put on them their clothes, and they set him thereon. JOHN xii. 17.— The people therefore that was with him when he called Lazarus out of his grave, and raised him from the dead, bare record. MARK xi. 8.—And a very great multitude spread their garments in the way; (MAT. xxi. 8, 9,) others cut down branches from the trees, and strewed them in the way; and they that went before, and that followed, cried, saying, Hosanna to the Son of David: Blessed is he that cometh in the name of the Lord; Hosanna in the highest.

LUKE xix. 39–44.—And some of the Pharisees from among the multitude said unto him, Master, rebuke thy disciples. And he answered and said unto them, I tell you that, if these should hold their peace, the stones would immediately cry out. And when he was come near, he beheld the city, and wept over it, saying, If thou hadst known, even thou, at least in this thy day, the things which belong unto thy peace! but now they are hid from thine eyes. For the days shall come upon thee, that thine enemies shall cast a trench about thee, and compass thee round, and keep thee in on every side, and shall lay thee even with the ground, and thy children within thee; and they shall not leave in thee one stone upon another; because thou knewest not the time of thy visitation.

MAT. xxi. 10-13.—And when he was come into Jerusalem, all the city was moved, saying, Who is this? And the multitude said, This is Jesus the prophet of Nazareth of Galilee. And Jesus went into the temple of God, and cast out all them that sold and bought in the temple, and overthrew the tables of the money changers, and the seats of them that sold doves, And said unto them, It is written, My house shall be called the house of prayer; but ye have made it a den of thieves. LUKE xx. 1, 2.—Then the chief priests and the scribes came upon him with the elders, and spake unto him, saying, Tell us, by what authority doest thou these things? or who is he that gave thee this authority? MARK xi. 29.—And Jesus answered and said unto them, I will also ask of you one question, and answer me, and I will tell you by what authority I do these things. LUKE xx. 4-6.— The baptism of John, was it from heaven, or of men? And they reasoned with themselves, saying, If we shall say, From heaven; he will say, Why then believed ye him not? But and if we say, Of men; all the people will stone us: for they be persuaded that John was a prophet. MAT. xxi. 27, 28.—And they answered Jesus, and said, We cannot tell. And he said unto them, Neither tell I you by what authority I do these things. But what think ye? MAT. xxi. 33, 34.—There was a certain householder, which planted a vineyard, and set a hedge about it, and digged a place for the winefat, and built a tower, and let it out to husbandmen, and went into a far country. And when the time of the fruit drew near, (LUKE xx. 10,) he sent a servant to the husbandmen, that they should give him of the fruit of the vineyard: but the husbandmen beat him, and sent him away empty. MARK xii. 4–6.—And again he sent unto them another servant; and at him they cast stones, and wounded him in the head, and sent him away shamefully handled. And again he sent another; and him they killed, and many others; beating some, and killing some. Having yet therefore one son, his well beloved, (LUKE xx. 13–15,) then said the lord of the vineyard, What shall I do? I will send my beloved son: it may be they will reverence him when they see him. But when the husbandmen saw him, they reasoned among themselves, saying, This is the heir: come, let us kill him, that the inheritance may be ours. So they cast him out of the vineyard, and killed him. MAT. xxi. 40–44.—When the lord therefore of the vineyard cometh, what will he do unto those husbandmen? They say unto him, He will miserably destroy those wicked men, and will let out his vineyard unto other husbandmen, which shall render him the fruits in their seasons. Jesus saith unto them, Did ye never read in the Scriptures, The stone which the builders rejected, the same is become the head of the corner: this is the Lord's doing, and it is marvellous in our eyes? Therefore say I unto you, The kingdom of God shall be taken from you, and given to a nation bringing forth the fruits thereof. And whosoever shall fall on this stone shall be broken: but on whomsoever it shall fall, it will grind him to powder. MAT. xxiii. 37–39.—O Jerusalem, Jerusalem, thou that killest the prophets, and stonest them which are sent unto thee, how often would I have gathered thy children together, even as a hen gathereth her chickens under her wings, and ye would not! Behold, your house is left unto you desolate. For I say unto you, Ye shall not see me henceforth, till ye shall say, Blessed is he that cometh in the name of the Lord.

MAT. xxi. 45, 46.—And when the chief priests and Pharisees had heard his parables, they perceived that he spake of them. But when they sought to lay hands on him, they feared the multitude, (MARK xii. 12,) and they left him, and went their way.

Then may follow a short address, based upon the portion of Scripture read, after which the congregation shall sing a hymn.
Then shall the Minister say:

He was wounded for our transgressions.

The Congregation shall answer:

He was bruised for our iniquities.

Minister.

Let us love him.

Congregation.

Because he first loved us.

The Minister shall offer a suitable prayer, after which the service may conclude with a Doxology and the Benediction.

Second Service.

WITH everlasting kindness will I have mercy on thee, saith the Lord thy Redeemer.—ISA. liv. 8. He that eateth my flesh, and drinketh my blood, dwelleth in me, and I in him; he hath eternal life, and I will raise him up at the last day.—JOHN vi. 54–56.

HEAR to day the second part of the history of the Passion of our Lord, as it is written by the four Evangelists. It contains the account of the preparation of the passover; the strife among the disciples as to which of them should be accounted the greatest, and the washing of the apostles' feet; the pointing out by Jesus of the traitor and his warning to Peter; and closes with the institution of the holy Supper. It reads thus:

LUKE xxii. 7–11.—Then came the day of unleavened bread, when the passover must be killed. And he sent Peter and John, saying, Go and prepare us the passover, that we may eat. And they said unto him, Where wilt thou that we prepare? And he said unto them, Behold, when ye are entered into the city, there shall a man meet you, bearing a pitcher of water; follow him into the house where he entereth in. And ye shall say unto the goodman of the house, The Master saith unto thee, (MAT. xxvi. 18,) My time is at hand; I will keep the passover at thy house with my disciples. LUKE xxii. 12.—And he shall show you a large upper room furnished: there make ready. MARK xiv. 16, 17.—And his disciples went forth, and came into the city, and found as he had said unto them: and they made ready the passover. Now when the even was come, he sat down with the twelve. LUKE xxii. 15–18.—And he said unto them, With desire I have desired to eat this passover with you before I suffer: For I say unto you, I will not any more eat thereof, until it be fulfilled in the kingdom of God. And he took the cup, and gave thanks, and said, Take this, and divide it among yourselves: For I say unto you, I will not drink henceforth of this fruit of the vine, until that day when I drink it new with you in my Father's kingdom.

LUKE xxii. 24–30.—And there was also a strife among them, which of them should be accounted the greatest. And he said unto them, The kings of the Gentiles exercise lordship over them; and they that exercise authority upon them are called benefactors. But ye shall not be so: but he that is greatest among you, let him be as the younger; and he that is chief, as he that doth serve. For whether is greater, he that sitteth at meat, or he that serveth? is not he that sitteth at meat? but I am among you as he that serveth. Ye are they which have continued with me in my temptations. And I appoint unto you a kingdom, as my Father hath appointed unto me; that ye may eat and drink at my table in my kingdom, and sit on thrones judging the twelve tribes of Israel.

JOHN xiii. 2–17.—And supper being ended, the devil having now put into the heart of Judas Iscariot, Simon's son, to betray him; Jesus knowing that the Father had given all things into his hands, and that he was come from God, and went to God; he riseth from supper, and laid aside his garments; and took a towel, and girded himself. After that he poureth water into a basin, and began to wash the disciples' feet, and to wipe them with the towel wherewith he was girded. Then cometh he to Simon Peter: and Peter saith unto him, Lord, dost thou wash my feet? Jesus answered and said unto him, What I do thou knowest not now; but thou shalt know hereafter. Peter saith unto him, Thou shalt never wash my feet. Jesus answered him, If I wash thee not, thou hast no part with me. Simon Peter saith unto him, Lord, not my feet only, but also my hands and my head. Jesus saith to him, He that is washed needeth not save to wash his feet, but is clean every whit: and ye are clean, but not all. For he knew who should betray him; therefore said he, Ye are not all clean. So after he had washed their feet, and had taken his garments, and was set down again, he said unto them, Know ye what I have done to you? Ye call me Master and Lord: and ye say well; for so I am. If I then, your Lord and Master, have washed your feet; ye also ought to wash one another's feet. For I have given you an example, that ye should do as I have done to you. Verily, verily, I say unto you, The servant is not greater than his lord; neither he that is sent greater than he that sent him. If ye know these things, happy are ye if ye do them.

JOHN xiii. 21, 22.—When Jesus had thus said, he was troubled in spirit, and testified, and said, Verily, verily, I say unto you, that one of you shall betray me. Then the disciples looked one on another, doubting of whom he spake. And they began to be sorrowful, and to say unto him one by one, Is it I? and another said, Is it I? And he answered and said unto them, It is one of the twelve, that dippeth with me in the dish. The Son of man indeed goeth, as it is written of him: but woe to that man by whom the Son of man is betrayed! good were it for that man if he had never been born. MAT. xxvi. 25.—Then Judas, which betrayed him, answered and said, Master, is it I? He said unto him, Thou hast said. JOHN xiii. 23–30.—Now there was leaning on Jesus' bosom one of his disciples, whom Jesus loved. Simon Peter therefore beckoned to him, that he should ask who it should be of whom he spake. He then lying on Jesus' breast saith unto him, Lord, who is it? Jesus answered, He it is, to whom I shall give a sop, when I have dipped it. And when he had dipped the sop, he gave it to Judas Iscariot, the son of Simon. And after the sop Satan entered into him. Then said Jesus unto him, That thou doest, do quickly. Now no man at the table knew for what intent he spake this unto him. For some of them thought, because Judas had the bag, that Jesus had said unto him, Buy those things that we have need of against the feast; or, that he should give something to the poor. He then, having received the sop, went immediately out; and it was night. LUKE xxii. 31–34.—And the Lord said, Simon, Simon, behold, Satan hath desired to have you, that he may sift you as wheat; but I have prayed for thee, that thy faith fail not: and when thou art converted, strengthen thy brethren. And he said unto him, Lord, I am ready to go with thee, both into prison, and to death. And he said, I tell thee, Peter, the cock shall not crow this day, before that thou shalt thrice deny that thou knowest me.

MARK xiv. 22.—And as they did eat, Jesus took bread, and blessed, and brake it, and gave to them, and said, Take, eat; this is my body, (LUKE xxii. 19,) which is given for you: this do in remembrance of me. 1 COR. xi. 25.—After the same manner also he took the cup, when he had supped, (MAT. xxvi. 27,) and gave thanks, and gave it to them, saying, Drink ye all of it: (1 COR. xi. 25,) This cup is the new testament in my blood, (LUKE xxii. 20,) which is shed for many for the remission of sins, (1 COR. xi. 25,) this do ye, as oft as ye drink it, in remembrance of me. MARK xiv. 23.—And they all drank of it.

MARK xiv. 26.—And when they had sung a hymn, they went out into the mount of Olives.

Third Service.

PRAISE and thanksgiving be unto him, who gave himself for us, that he might redeem us from all iniquity, and purify unto himself a peculiar people, zealous of good works.—TIT. ii. 14. He hath an unchangeable priesthood. Wherefore he is able also to save them to the uttermost that come unto God by him, seeing he ever liveth to make intercession for them.—HEB. vii. 24, 25.

HEAR to-day the third part of the history of the Passion of our Lord, as it is written by the four Evangelists. It contains Jesus' intercessory prayer, his agony in the garden of Gethsemane, and his being taken captive.

It reads thus:

JOHN xvii.—These words spake Jesus, and lifted up his eyes to heaven, and said, Father, the hour is come; glorify thy Son, that thy Son also may glorify thee: as thou hast given him power over all flesh, that he should give eternal life to as many as thou hast given him. And this is life eternal, that they might know thee the only true God, and Jesus Christ whom thou hast sent. I have glorified thee on the earth: I have finished the work which thou gavest me to do. And now, O Father, glorify thou me with thine own self with the glory which I had with thee before the world was. I have manifested thy name unto the men which thou gavest me out of the world: thine they were, and thou gavest them me; and they have kept thy word. Now they have known that all things whatsoever thou hast given me are of thee. For I have given unto them the words which thou gavest me; and they have received them, and have known surely that I came out from thee, and they have believed that thou didst send me. I pray for them: 1 pray not for the world, but for them which thou hast given me; for they are thine. And all mine are thine, and thine are mine; and I am glorified in them. And now I am no more in the world, but these are in the world, and I come to thee. Holy Father, keep through thine own name those whom thou hast given me, that they may be one, as we are. While I was with them in the world, I kept them in thy name: those that thou gavest me I have kept, and none of them is lost, but the son of perdition; that the scripture might be fulfilled. And now come I to thee; and these things I speak in the world, that they might have my joy fulfilled in themselves. I have given them thy word; and the world hath hated them, because they are not of the world, even as I am not of the world. I pray not that thou shouldst take them out of the world, but that thou shouldst keep them from the evil. They are not of the world, even as I am not of the world. Sanctify them through thy truth: thy word is truth. As thou hast sent me into the world, even so have I also sent them into the world. And for their sakes I sanctify myself, that they also might be sanctified through the truth. Neither pray I for these alone, but for them also which shall believe on me through their word; that they all may be one; as thou, Father, art in me, and I in thee, that they also may be one in us: that the world may believe that thou hast sent me. And the glory which thou gavest me I have given them; that they may be one, even as we are one: I in them, and thou in me, that they may be made perfect in one; and that the world may know that thou hast sent me, and hast loved them, as thou hast loved me. Father, I will that they also, whom thou hast given me, be with me where I am; that they may behold my glory, which thou has given me: for thou lovedst me before the foundation of the world. O righteous Father, the world hath not known thee: but I have known thee, and these have known that thou hast sent me. And I have declared unto them thy name, and will declare it; that the love wherewith thou hast loved me may be in them, and I in them.

JOHN xviii. 1.—When Jesus had spoken these words, he went forth with his disciples over the brook Cedron. MARK xiv. 32.—And they came to a place which was named Gethsemane: (JOHN xviii. 1,) where was a garden, into the which he entered, and his disciples. Mat. xxvi. 36–38.—And he said unto them, Sit ye here, while I go and pray yonder. And he took with him Peter and the two sons of Zebedee, and began to be sorrowful and very heavy. Then saith he unto them, My soul is exceeding sorrowful even unto death: tarry ye here, and watch with me. Luke xxii. 41.—And he was withdrawn from them about a stone's cast, (Mat. xxvi. 39–43,) and fell on his face, and prayed, saying, O my Father, if it be possible, let this cup pass from me: nevertheless, not as I will, but as thou wilt. And he cometh unto the disciples, and findeth them asleep, and saith unto Peter, What, could ye not watch with me one hour? Watch and pray, that ye enter not into temptation: the spirit indeed is willing, but the flesh is weak. He went away again the second time, and prayed, saying, O my Father, if this cup may not pass away from me, except I drink it, thy will be done. And he came and found them asleep again: for their eyes were heavy, (Mark xiv. 40,) neither wist they what to answer him. Mat. xxvi. 44.—And he left them, and went away again, and prayed the third time, (Luke xxii. 42–46,) saying, Father, if thou be willing, remove this cup from me: nevertheless, not my will, but thine, be done. And there appeared an angel unto him from heaven, strengthening him. And being in an agony he prayed more earnestly: and his sweat was as it were great drops of blood falling down to the ground. And when he rose up from prayer, and was come to his disciples, he found them sleeping for sorrow, and said unto them, (Mat. xxvi. 45, 46,) Sleep on now, and take your rest: behold, the hour is at hand, and the Son of man is betrayed into the hands of sinners. Rise, let us be going: behold, he is at hand that doth betray me.

MAT. xxvi. 47, 48.—And while he yet spake, lo, Judas, one of the twelve, came, and with him a great multitude with swords and staves, from the chief priests and elders of the people. Now he that betrayed him gave them a sign, saying, Whomsoever I shall kiss, that same is he : hold him fast. JOHN xviii. 4–9. Jesus therefore, knowing all things that should come upon him, went forth, and said unto them, Whom seek ye? They answered him, Jesus of Nazareth. Jesus said unto them, I am he. And Judas also, which betrayed him, stood with them. As soon then as he had said unto them, I am he, they went backward, and fell to the ground. Then asked he them again, Whom seek ye? And they said, Jesus of Nazareth. Jesus answered, I have told you that I am he : if therefore ye seek me, let these go their way : that the saying might be fulfilled, which he spake, Of them which thou gavest me have I lost none. MAT. xxvi. 49.—And forthwith he (Judas) came to Jesus, and said, Hail, Master; and kissed him. LUKE xxii. 48–50.—But Jesus said unto him, Judas, betrayest thou the Son of man with a kiss? When they which were about him saw what would follow, they said unto him, Lord, shall we smite with the sword? And one of them, (JOHN xviii. 10,) Simon Peter, having a sword, drew it, and smote the high priest's servant, and cut off his right ear. The servant's name was Malchus. LUKE xxii. 51.—And Jesus touched his ear, and healed him. MAT. xxvi. 52–55.—Then said Jesus unto him, (Peter,) Put up again thy sword into his place : for all they that take the sword shall perish with the sword. Thinkest thou that I cannot now pray to my Father, and he shall presently give me more than twelve legions of angels? But how then shall the Scriptures be fulfilled, that thus it must be? In that same hour said

Jesus to the multitudes, Are ye come out as against a thief with swords and staves for to take me? I sat daily with you teaching in the temple, and ye laid no hold on me. LUKE xxii. 53.—But this is your hour, and the power of darkness. MAT. xxvi. 56–58.—But all this was done, that the scriptures of the prophets might be fulfilled. Then all the disciples forsook him, and fled. And they that had laid hold on Jesus led him away to Caiaphas the high priest, where the scribes and the elders were assembled. But Peter followed him afar off unto the high priest's palace.

Fourth Service.

BEHOLD, the hour cometh, yea, is now come, that ye shall be scattered every man to his own, and shall leave me alone; and yet I am not alone, because the Father is with me.—JOHN xvi. 32. Let this mind be in you, which was also in Christ Jesus; he humbled himself, and became obedient unto death, even the death of the cross.—PHIL. ii. 5, 8.

HEAR to-day the fourth part of the history of the Passion of our Lord. It contains his examination before Annas and Caiaphas; Peter's denial; the departure from the council, and the remorse of Judas. It reads thus:

JOHN xviii. 12–14, 19–24.—Then the band and the captain and officers of the Jews took Jesus, and bound him, and led him away to Annas first; for he was father-in-law to Caiaphas, which was the high priest that same year. Now Caiaphas was he, which gave counsel to the Jews, that it was expedient that one man should die for the people. The high priest then asked Jesus of his disciples, and of his doctrine. Jesus answered him, I spake openly to the world; I ever taught in the synagogue, and in the temple, whither the Jews always resort; and in secret have I said nothing. Why askest thou me? ask them which heard me, what I have said unto them: behold, they know what I said. And when he had thus spoken, one of the officers which stood by struck Jesus with the palm of his hand, saying, Answerest thou the high priest so? Jesus answered him, If I have spoken evil, bear witness of the evil: but if well, why smitest thou me? Now Annas had sent him bound unto Caiaphas the high priest. MAT. xxvi. 57.—And they that had laid hold on Jesus led him away to Caiaphas the high priest, (MARK xiv. 53,) and with him were assembled all the chief priests and the elders and the scribes. JOHN xviii. 15.—And Simon Peter followed Jesus, and so did another disciple: that disciple was known unto the high priest, and went in with Jesus into the palace of the high priest. MAT. xxvi. 59–60.—Now the chief priests, and elders, and all the council, sought false witness against Jesus to put him to death; but found none: yea, though many false witnesses came, yet found they none; (MARK xiv. 56,) their witness agreed not together. MAT. xxvi. 60, 61.—At the last came two false witnesses, and said, This fellow said, I am able to destroy the temple of God, and to build it in three days. MARK xiv. 60, 61. —And the high priest stood up in the midst, and asked Jesus, saying, Answerest thou nothing? what is it which these witness against thee? But he held his peace, and answered nothing. Again the high priest asked him, and said unto him, Art thou the Christ, the Son of the Blessed? MAT. xxvi. 63–68. —I adjure thee by the living God, that thou tell us whether thou be the Christ, the Son of God. Jesus saith unto him, Thou hast said: nevertheless I say unto you, Hereafter shall ye see the Son of man sitting on the right hand of power, and coming in the clouds of heaven. Then the high priest rent his clothes, saying, He hath spoken blasphemy; what further need have we of witnesses? behold, now ye have heard his blasphemy. What think ye? They answered and said, He is guilty of death. Then did they spit in his face, and buffeted him; and others smote him with the palms of their hands, saying, Prophesy unto us, thou Christ, Who is he that smote thee?

JOHN xviii. 16, 17.—But Peter stood at the door without. Then went out that other disciple, which was known unto the high priest, and spake unto her that kept the door, and brought in Peter. Then saith the damsel that kept the door unto Peter, Art not thou also one of this man's disciples? He saith, I am not; (MAT. xxvi. 58,) and went in, and sat with the servants, to see the end. JOHN xviii. 18.—And the servants and officers stood there, who had made a fire of coals, for it was cold; and they warmed themselves: and Peter stood with them, and warmed himself. MARK xiv. 66, 67.—And as Peter was beneath in the palace, there cometh one of the maids of the high priest: and when she saw Peter warming himself, she looked upon him, and said, And thou also wast with Jesus of Nazareth. MAT. xxvi. 70.—But he denied before them all, (MARK xiv. 68,) saying, I know not, neither understand I what thou sayest. And he went out into the porch; and the cock crew. LUKE xxii. 59. And about the space of one hour after another confidently affirmed, saying, Of a truth this fellow also was with him; for he is a Galilean. JOHN xviii. 26.—One of the servants of the high priest, being his kinsman whose ear Peter cut off, saith, Did not I see thee in the garden with him? MAT. xxvi. 73, 74.—

And after a while came unto him they that stood by, and said to Peter, Surely thou also art one of them; for thy speech bewrayeth thee. Then began he to curse and to swear, (MARK xiv. 71,) I know not this man of whom ye speak. LUKE xxii. 60.—And immediately, while he yet spake, the cock crew (MARK. xiv. 72,) the second time. LUKE xxii. 61.—And the Lord turned and looked upon Peter. MARK xiv. 72.—And Peter called to mind the word that Jesus said unto him, Before the cock crow twice, thou shalt deny me thrice. LUKE xxii. 62—And Peter went out, and wept bitterly.

MAT. xxvii. 1.—When the morning was come, all the chief priests and elders of the people took counsel against Jesus to put him to death : (LUKE xxii. 66 ; xxiii. 1;) and led him into their council, saying, art thou the Christ? tell us. And he said unto them, If I tell you, ye will not believe : and if I also ask you, ye will not answer me, nor let me go. Hereafter shall the Son of man sit on the right hand of the power of God. Then said they all, Art thou then the Son of God? And he said unto them, Ye say that I am. And they said, What need we any further witness? for we ourselves have heard of his own mouth. And the whole multitude of them arose, (MARK xv. 1,) and bound Jesus, and carried him away, (JOHN xviii. 28,) from Caiaphas unto the hall of judgment, (MAT. xxvii. 2,) and delivered him to Pontius Pilate the governor. JOHN xviii. 28.—And it was early; and they themselves went not into the judgment hall, lest they should be defiled ; but that they might eat the passover.

MAT. xxvii. 3–10.—Then Judas, which had betrayed him, when he saw that he was condemned, repented himself, and brought again the thirty pieces of silver to the chief priests and elders, saying, I have sinned in that I have betrayed the innocent blood. And they said, What is that to us? see thou to that. And he cast down the pieces of silver in the temple, and departed, and went and hanged himself. And the chief priests took the silver pieces, and said, It is not lawful for to put them into the treasury, because it is the price of blood. And they took counsel, and bought with them the potter's field, to bury strangers in. Wherefore that field was called, The field of blood, unto this day. Then was fulfilled that which was spoken by Jeremy the prophet, saying, And they took the thirty pieces of silver, the price of him that was valued, whom they of the children of Israel did value; and gave them for the potter's field, as the Lord appointed me.

Fifth Service.

BUT he was wounded for our transgressions, he was bruised for our iniquities; the chastisement of our peace was upon him; and with his stripes we are healed.—ISA. liii. 5. I give thee charge in the sight of God, who quickeneth all things, and before Christ Jesus, who before Pontius Pilate witnessed a good confession; that thou keep this commandment without spot, unrebukable, until the appearing of our Lord Jesus Christ.—1 TIM. vi. 13, 14.

HEAR to-day the fifth part of the history of the Passion of our Lord. It presents Jesus before Pilate and Herod; Pilate causes Jesus to be scourged, but desires to release him; finally he releases Barabbas and delivers Jesus up to be crucified.

It reads thus:

JOHN xviii. 29-32.—Pilate then went out unto them, and said, What accusation bring ye against this man? They answered and said unto him, If he were not a malefactor, we would not have delivered him up unto thee. Then said Pilate unto them, Take ye him, and judge him according to your law. The Jews therefore said unto him, It is not lawful for us to put any man to death: that the saying of Jesus might be fulfilled, which he spake, signifying what death he should die. LUKE xxiii. 2.—And they began to accuse him, saying, We found this fellow perverting the nation, and forbidding to give tribute to Cesar, saying that he himself is Christ a king. JOHN xviii. 33-38.—Then Pilate entered into the judgment hall again, and called Jesus, and said unto him, Art thou the King of the Jews? Jesus answered him, Sayest thou this thing of thyself, or did others tell it thee of me? Pilate answered, Am I a Jew? Thine own nation and the chief priests have delivered thee unto me: what hast thou done? Jesus answered, My kingdom is not of this world: if my kingdom were of this world, then would my servants fight, that I should not be delivered to the Jews: but now is my kingdom not from hence. Pilate therefore said unto him, Art thou a king then? Jesus answered, Thou sayest that I am a king. To this end was I born, and for this cause came I into the world, that I should bear witness unto the truth. Every one that is of the truth heareth my voice. Pilate saith unto him, What is truth? And when he had said this, he went out again unto the Jews, and saith unto them, I find in him no fault at all. MAT. xxvii. 12-14.—And when he was accused of the chief priests and elders, he answered nothing. Then said Pilate unto him, Hearest thou not how many things they witness against thee? And he answered him to never a word; insomuch

that the governor marvelled greatly. LUKE xxiii. 5.—
And they were the more fierce, saying, He stirreth up
the people, teaching throughout all Jewry, beginning
from Galilee to this place.

LUKE xxiii. 6–16.—When Pilate heard of Galilee,
he asked whether the man were a Galilean. And as
soon as he knew that he belonged unto Herod's juris-
diction, he sent him to Herod, who himself also was
at Jerusalem at that time. And when Herod saw
Jesus, he was exceeding glad : for he was desirous to
see him of a long season, because he had heard many
things of him; and he hoped to have seen some miracle
done by him. Then he questioned with him in many
words; but he answered him nothing. And the chief
priests and scribes stood and vehemently accused him.
And Herod with his men of war set him at nought,
and mocked him, and arrayed him in a gorgeous robe,
and sent him again to Pilate. And the same day
Pilate and Herod were made friends together; for
before they were at enmity between themselves.
And Pilate, when he had called together the chief
priests and the rulers and the people, said unto them,
Ye have brought this man unto me, as one that per-
verteth the people; and, behold, I having examined him
before you, have found no fault in this man touching
those things whereof ye accuse him : no, nor yet
Herod : for I sent you to him; and, lo, nothing worthy
of death is done unto him. I will therefore chastise
him, and release him.

MAT. xxvii. 15, 16.—Now at that feast the governor
was wont to release unto the people a prisoner, whom
they would. And they had then a notable prisoner,
called Barabbas, (LUKE xxiii. 25,) that for sedition
and murder was cast into prison. MARK xv. 8, 9.—

And the multitude crying aloud began to desire him to do as he had ever done unto them. But Pilate answered them, saying, (MAT. xxvii. 17, 18,) Whom will ye that I release unto you? Barabbas, or Jesus which is called Christ? MARK xv. 10.—For he knew that the chief priests had delivered him for envy. MAT. xxvii. 19.—When he was set down on the judgment seat, his wife sent unto him, saying, Have thou nothing to do with that just man : for I have suffered many things this day in a dream because of him. MARK xv. 11, 12.—But the chief priests moved the people, that he should rather release Barabbas unto them. And Pilate answered and said again unto them, What will ye then that I shall do unto him whom ye call the King of the Jews? LUKE xxiii. 21, 22.—But they cried, saying, Crucify him, crucify him. And he said unto them the third time, Why, what evil hath he done? I have found no cause of death in him : I will therefore chastise him, and let him go. MARK xv. 14.—And they cried out the more exceedingly, Crucify him. LUKE xxiii. 23.—And the voices of them and of the chief priests prevailed. JOHN xix. 1.—Then Pilate therefore took Jesus, and scourged him. MARK xv. 16.—And the soldiers led him away into the hall, called Pretorium; and they call together the whole band. MAT. xxvii. 28, 29.— And they stripped him, and put on him a scarlet robe. And when they had platted a crown of thorns, they put it upon his head, and a reed in his right hand : and they bowed the knee before him, and mocked him, saying: (JOHN xix. 3-12,) Hail, King of the Jews! and they smote him with their hands. Pilate therefore went forth again, and saith unto them, Behold, I bring him forth to you, that ye may know that I find no fault in him. Then came Jesus forth, wearing the crown of thorns, and the purple robe. And Pilate saith unto them, Behold the man! When the chief priests therefore and officers saw him, they cried out, saying, Crucify him, crucify him. Pilate saith unto them, Take ye him, and crucify him: for I find no fault in him. The Jews answered him, We have a law, and by our law he ought to die, because he made himself the Son of God. When Pilate therefore heard that saying, he was the more afraid; and went again into the judgment hall, and saith unto Jesus, Whence art thou? But Jesus gave him no answer. Then saith Pilate unto him, Speakest thou not unto me? knowest thou not that I have power to crucify thee, and have power to release thee? Jesus answered, Thou couldest have no power at all against me, except it were given thee from above: therefore he that delivered me unto thee hath the greater sin. And from thenceforth Pilate sought to release him.

JOHN xix. 12–15.—But the Jews cried out, saying, If thou let this man go, thou art not Cesar's friend: whosoever maketh himself a king speaketh against Cesar. When Pilate therefore heard that saying, he brought Jesus forth, and sat down in the judgment seat in a place that is called the Pavement, but in the Hebrew, Gabbatha. And it was the preparation of the passover, and about the sixth hour: and he saith unto the Jews, Behold your King! But they cried out, Away with him, away with him, crucify him. Pilate saith unto them, Shall I crucify your King? The chief priests answered, We have no king but Cesar. MAT. xxvii. 24–26.—When Pilate saw that he could prevail nothing, but that rather a tumult was made, he took water, and washed his hands before the multitude, saying, I am innocent of the blood of this just person: see ye to it. Then answered all the people, and said, His blood be on us, and on our children. Then released he Barabbas unto them: and when he had scourged Jesus, he delivered him to be crucified.

Sixth Service.

BEHOLD the Lamb of God, which taketh away the sin of the world.—JOHN i. 29. Who his own self bare our sins in his own body on the tree, that we, being dead to sins, should live unto righteousness: by whose stripes ye were healed.—1 PET. ii. 24.

HEAR to-day the sixth part of the history of the Passion of our Lord. It presents to us, Jesus going to Golgotha to be crucified, and his crucifixion and death.
It reads thus:

MAT. xxvii. 27, 31.—Then the soldiers of the governor took Jesus, and took the robe off from him, and put his own raiment on him, and led him away to crucify him. LUKE xxiii. 32.—And there were also two others, malefactors, led with him to be put to death. JOHN xix. 17.—And he bore his cross. MAT. xxvii. 32.—And as they came out, they found a man of Cyrene, Simon by name: him they compelled to bear his cross; (LUKE xxiii. 26-31;) and on him they laid the cross, that he might bear it after Jesus. And there followed him a great company of people, and of women, which also bewailed and lamented him. But Jesus turning unto them said, Daughters of Jerusalem, weep not for me, but weep for yourselves, and for your children. For, behold, the days are coming, in the which they shall say, Blessed are the barren, and the wombs that never bare, and the paps which never gave suck. Then shall they begin to say to the mountains, Fall on us; and to the hills, Cover us. For if they do these things in a green tree, what shall be done in the dry?

Mat. xxvii. 33.—And when they were come unto a place called Golgotha, that is to say, a place of a skull, (Mark xv. 23,) they gave him to drink wine mingled with myrrh: but he received it not. There they crucified him, and the malefactors, one on the right hand, and the other on the left. Luke xxiii. 34.—Then said Jesus, Father, forgive them; for they know not what they do. Mark xv. 25.—And it was the third hour. John xix. 19-24.—And Pilate wrote a title, and put it on the cross. And the writing was, JESUS OF NAZARETH THE KING OF THE JEWS. This title then read many of the Jews; for the place where Jesus was crucified was nigh to the city: and it was written in Hebrew, and Greek, and Latin. Then said the chief priests of the Jews to Pilate, Write not, The King of the Jews; but that he said, I am King of the Jews. Pilate answered, What I have written I have written. Then the soldiers, when they had crucified Jesus, took his garments, and made four parts, to every soldier a part; and also his coat: now the coat was without seam, woven from the top throughout. They said therefore among themselves, Let us not rend it, but cast lots for it, whose it shall be: that the scripture might be fulfilled, which saith, They parted my raiment among them, and for my vesture they did cast lots. These things therefore the soldiers did. Mat. xxvii. 36.—And sitting down they watched him there; (Luke xxiii. 35;) and the people stood beholding. John xix. 25-27.—Now there stood by the cross of Jesus his mother, and his mother's sister, Mary the wife of Cleophas, and Mary Magdalene. When Jesus therefore saw his mother, and the disciple standing by, whom he loved, he saith unto his mother, Woman, behold thy son! Then saith he to the disciple, Behold thy mother! And from that hour that disciple took her unto his own home.

MAT. xxvii. 39.—And they that passed by reviled him, wagging their heads, (MARK xv. 29, 30,) and saying, Ah, thou that destroyest the temple, and buildest it in three days, save thyself. MATT. xxvii. 40–44.—If thou be the Son of God, come down from the cross. Likewise also the chief priests mocking him, with the scribes and elders, said, He saved others; himself he cannot save. If he be the King of Israel, let him now come down from the cross, and we will believe him. He trusted in God; let him deliver him now, if he will have him: for he said, I am the Son of God. The thieves also, which were crucified with him, cast the same in his teeth. LUKE xxiii. 39–43. —And one of the malefactors which were hanged railed on him, saying, If thou be Christ, save thyself and us. But the other answering rebuked him, saying, Dost not thou fear God, seeing thou art in the same condemnation? And we indeed justly; for we receive the due reward of our deeds: but this man hath done nothing amiss. And he said unto Jesus, Lord, remember me when thou comest into thy kingdom. And Jesus said unto him, Verily I say unto thee, To-day shalt thou be with me in paradise.

LUKE xxiii. 44, 45.—And it was about the sixth hour, and there was a darkness over all the earth until the ninth hour. And the sun was darkened. MAT. xxvii. 46.—And about the ninth hour Jesus cried with a loud voice, saying, Eli, Eli, lama sabachthani? that is to say, My God, my God, why hast thou forsaken me? MARK xv. 35.—And some of them that stood by, when they heard it, said, Behold, he calleth Elias. JOHN xix. 28, 29.—After this, Jesus knowing that all things were now accomplished, that the scripture might be fulfilled, saith, I thirst. Now there was set a vessel full of vinegar. MAT. xxvii. 48, 49.—And straightway one of them ran, and took a sponge, and filled it with vinegar, and put it on a reed, and gave him to drink. The rest said, Let be, let us see whether Elias will come to save him. JOHN xix. 30.—When Jesus therefore had received the vinegar, he said, It is finished. LUKE xxiii. 46.—And when Jesus had cried with a loud voice, he said, Father, into thy hands I commend my spirit: and having said thus, (JOHN xix. 30,) he bowed his head, and gave up the ghost.

MAT. xxvii. 51-54.—And, behold, the vail of the temple was rent in twain from the top to the bottom; and the earth did quake, and the rocks rent; and the graves were opened; and many bodies of the saints which slept arose, and came out of the graves after his resurrection, and went into the holy city, and appeared unto many. MARK xv. 39.—And when the centurion, which stood over against him, saw that he so cried out, and gave up the ghost, (LUKE xxiii. 47,) he glorified God, saying, Certainly this was a righteous man. MARK xv. 39.—Truly this man was the Son of God. MAT. xxvii. 54. Now when they that were with him, watching Jesus, saw the earthquake, and those things that were done, they feared greatly, saying, Truly this was the Son of God. LUKE xxiii. 48. —And all the people that came together to that sight, beholding the things which were done, smote their breasts, and returned.

Seventh Service.

AND his rest shall be glorious.—ISA. xi. 10. Worthy is the lamb that was slain to receive power and riches, and wisdom, and strength, and honor, and glory, and blessing.—REV. v. 12.

HEAR to-day the close of the history of the Passion of our Lord. It presents to us the piercing of Jesus side, the burial, and the placing a watch over the grave.

It reads thus:

LUKE xxiii. 49.—And all his acquaintance, and the women that followed him from Galilee, stood afar off, beholding these things. MAT. xxvii. 56.—Among which was Mary Magdalene, and Mary the mother of James and Joses, and Salome the mother of Zebedee's children. MARK xv. 41.—Who also, when he was in Galilee, followed him, and ministered unto him; and many other women which came up with him unto Jerusalem.

JOHN xix. 31–37.—The Jews therefore, because it was the preparation, that the bodies should not remain upon the cross on the sabbath day, (for that sabbath day was a high day,) besought Pilate that their legs might be broken, and that they might be taken away. Then came the soldiers, and brake the legs of the first, and of the other which was crucified with him. But when they came to Jesus, and saw that he was dead already, they brake not his legs: but one of the soldiers with a spear pierced his side, and forthwith came there out blood and water. And he that saw it bare record, and his record is true; and he knoweth that he saith true, that ye might believe. For these things were done, that the scripture should be fulfilled, A bone of him shall not be broken. And again another scripture saith, They shall look on him whom they pierced.

MAT. xxvii. 57.—When the even was come, there came a rich man, (MARK xv. 43,) Joseph of Arimathea, an honorable counsellor, which also waited for the kingdom of God, (LUKE xxiii. 50, 51,) and he was a good man, and a just: The same had not consented to the counsel and deed of them: (JOHN xix. 38,) being a disciple of Jesus, but secretly for fear of the Jews. MARK xv. 43–46.—And he came, and went in boldly unto Pilate, and craved the body of Jesus. And Pilate marvelled if he were already dead: and calling unto him the centurion, he asked him whether he had been any while dead. And when he knew it of the centurion, he gave the body to Joseph. And he bought fine linen, and took him down. John xix. 39–41.—And there came also Nicodemus, (which at the first came to Jesus by night,) and brought a mixture of myrrh and aloes, about a hundred pounds weight. Then took they the body of Jesus, and wound it in linen clothes with the spices, as the manner of the Jews is to bury. Now in the place where he was crucified there was a garden; and in the garden a new sepulchre, (MAT. xxvii. 60,) which he had hewn out in the rock: (LUKE xxiii. 53,) wherein never man before was laid. JOHN xxix. 42.—There laid they Jesus therefore because of the Jews' preparation day; (MAT. xxvii. 60, 61,) and rolled a great stone to the door of the sepulchre, and departed. And there was Mary Magdalene, and the other Mary, sitting over against the sepulchre, (LUKE xxiii. 55, 56,) and beheld the sepulchre, and how his body was laid. And they returned, and prepared spices and ointments; and rested the sabbath day according to the commandment.

MAT. xxvii. 62–66.—Now the next day, that followed the day of the preparation, the chief priests and Pharisees came together unto Pilate, saying, Sir, we remember that that deceiver said, while he was yet alive, After three days I will rise again. Command therefore that the sepulchre be made sure until the third day, lest his disciples come by night, and steal him away, and say unto the people, He is risen from the dead: so the last error shall be worse than the first. Pilate said unto them, Ye have a watch: go your way, make it as sure as ye can. So they went, and made the sepulchre sure, sealing the stone, and setting a watch.

VIII.

The Epistles and Gospels

FOR THE

SUNDAYS AND FESTIVALS OF THE CHURCH-YEAR.

FIRST SUNDAY IN ADVENT.
Epistle, Rom. xiii. 11–14.
Gospel, Mat. xxi. 1–9.

SECOND SUNDAY IN ADVENT.
Epistle, Rom. xv. 4–13.
Gospel, Luke xxi. 25–36.

THIRD SUNDAY IN ADVENT.
Epistle, 1 Cor. iv. 1–5.
Gospel, Mat. xi. 2–10.

FOURTH SUNDAY IN ADVENT.
Epistle, Phil. iv. 4–7.
Gospel, John i. 19–28.

CHRISTMAS-DAY.
Epistle, Tit. ii. 11–14.
Or, Isa. ix. 2–7.
Gospel, Luke ii. 1–14.

SECOND CHRISTMAS-DAY.
Epistle, Tit. iii. 4–7.
Or, Acts vi. 8—vii. 1, 51–59.
Gospel, Luke ii. 15–20.

SUNDAY AFTER CHRISTMAS.
Epistle, Gal. iv. 1–7.
Gospel, Luke ii. 33–40.

CLOSE OF THE YEAR.
Epistle, 2 Tim. iv. 1–8.
Gospel, Luke xii. 35–40.

NEW YEAR'S-DAY.
Epistle, Gal. iii. 23–29.
Gospel, Luke ii. 21.

SUNDAY AFTER NEW-YEAR.
Epistle, 1 Pet iv. 12–19.
Gospel, Mat. ii. 13–23.

EPIPHANY.
Epistle, Isa. lx. 1–6.
Gospel, Mat. ii. 1–12.

FIRST SUNDAY AFTER EPIPHANY.
Epistle, Rom. xii. 1–6.
Gospel, Luke ii. 41–52.

SECOND SUNDAY AFTER EPIPHANY.
Epistle, Rom. xii. 7–16.
Gospel, John ii. 1–11.

THIRD SUNDAY AFTER EPIPHANY.
Epistle, Rom. xii. 17–21.
Gospel, Mat. viii. 1–13.

FOURTH SUNDAY AFTER EPIPHANY.
Epistle, Rom. xiii. 8–10.
Gospel, Mat. viii. 23–27.

FIFTH SUNDAY AFTER EPIPHANY.
Epistle, Col. iii. 12–17.
Gospel, Mat. xiii. 24–30.

SIXTH SUNDAY AFTER EPIPHANY.
Epistle, 2 Pet. i. 16–21.
Or, Col. iii. 18—iv. 1.
Gospel, Mat. xvii. 1–9.

THIRD SUNDAY BEFORE LENT.
Epistle, 1 Cor. ix. 24—x. 5.
Gospel, Mat. xx. 1–16.

THE EPISTLES AND GOSPELS. 143

SECOND SUNDAY BEFORE LENT.
Epistle, 2 Cor. xi. 19—xii. 9.
Gospel, Luke viii. 4–15.

SUNDAY BEFORE LENT.
Epistle, 1 Cor. xiii. 1–13.
Gospel, Luke xviii. 31–43.

FIRST SUNDAY IN LENT.
Epistle, 2 Cor. vi. 1–10.
Gospel, Mat. iv. 1–11.

SECOND SUNDAY IN LENT.
Epistle, 1 Thess. iv. 1–7.
Gospel, Mat. xv. 21–28.

THIRD SUNDAY IN LENT.
Epistle, Ephes. v. 1–9.
Gospel, Luke xi. 14–28.

FOURTH SUNDAY IN LENT.
Epistle, Gal. iv. 21–31.
Gospel, John vi. 1–15.

FIFTH SUNDAY IN LENT.
Epistle, Heb. ix. 11–15.
Gospel, John viii. 46–59.

SIXTH SUNDAY IN LENT.
Epistle, Phil. ii. 5–11.
    Or, 1 Cor. xi. 23–32.
Gospel, Mat. xxi. 1–9.

THURSDAY BEFORE EASTER.
Epistle, 1 Cor. xi. 23–32.
    Or, Exod. xii. 1–13.
Gospel, John xiii. 1–15.

GOOD FRIDAY.
Epistle, Isa. liii.
The Passion History.

EASTER SUNDAY.
Epistle, 1 Cor. v. 6–8.
Gospel, Mark xvi. 1–8.

EASTER MONDAY.
Epistle, Acts x. 34–41.
Gospel, Luke xxiv. 13–35.

FIRST SUNDAY AFTER EASTER.
Epistle, 1 John v. 4–10.
Gospel, John xx. 19–31.

SECOND SUNDAY AFTER EASTER.
Epistle, 1. Pet. ii. 21–25.
Gospel, John x. 12–16.

THIRD SUNDAY AFTER EASTER.
Epistle, 1 Pet. ii. 11–20.
Gospel, John xvi. 16–23.

FOURTH SUNDAY AFTER EASTER.
Epistle, James i. 16–21.
Gospel, John xvi. 5–15.

FIFTH SUNDAY AFTER EASTER.
Epistle, James i. 22–27.
Gospel, John xvi. 23–30.

ASCENSION-DAY.
Epistle, Acts i. 1–11.
Gospel, Mark xvi. 14–20.

SUNDAY AFTER ASCENSION.
Epistle, 1 Pet. iv. 8–11.
Gospel, John xv. 26—xvi. 4.

WHITSUNDAY.
Epistle, Acts ii. 1–13.
Gospel, John xiv. 23–31.

WHITMONDAY.
Epistle, Acts. x. 42–48.
Gospel, John iii. 16–21.

TRINITY SUNDAY.
Epistle, Rom. xi. 33–36.
Gospel, John iii. 1–15.

FIRST SUNDAY AFTER TRINITY.
Epistle, 1 John iv. 16–21.
Gospel, Luke xvi. 19–31.

SECOND SUNDAY AFTER TRINITY.
Epistle, 1 John iii. 13–18.
Gospel, Luke. xiv. 16–24.

THIRD SUNDAY AFTER TRINITY.
Epistle, 1 Pet. v. 6–11.
Gospel, Luke xv. 1–10.

FOURTH SUNDAY AFTER TRINITY.
Epistle, Rom. viii. 18–23.
Gospel, Luke vi. 36–42.

FIFTH SUNDAY AFTER TRINITY.
Epistle, 1 Pet. iii. 8–15.
Gospel, Luke v. 1–11.

SIXTH SUNDAY AFTER TRINITY.
Epistle, Rom. vi. 3–11.
Gospel, Mat. v. 20–26.

SEVENTH SUNDAY AFTER TRINITY.
Epistle, Rom. vi 19–23.
Gospel, Mark viii. 1–9.

EIGHTH SUNDAY AFTER TRINITY.
Epistle, Rom. viii. 12–17.
Gospel, Mat. vii. 15–23.

NINTH SUNDAY AFTER TRINITY.
Epistle, 1 Cor. x. 6–13.
Gospel, Luke xvi. 1–9.

TENTH SUNDAY AFTER TRINITY.
Epistle, 1 Cor. xii. 1–11.
Gospel, Luke xix. 41–48.

ELEVENTH SUNDAY AFTER TRINITY.
Epistle, 1 Cor. xv. 1–10.
Gospel, Luke xviii. 9–14.

TWELFTH SUNDAY AFTER TRINITY.
Epistle, 2 Cor. iii. 4–11.
Gospel, Mark vii. 31–37.

THIRTEENTH SUNDAY AFTER TRINITY.
Epistle, Gal. iii. 15–22.
Gospel, Luke. x. 23–37.

FOURTEENTH SUNDAY AFTER TRINITY.
Epistle, Gal. v. 16–24.
Gospel, Luke xvii. 11–19.

FIFTEENTH SUNDAY AFTER TRINITY.
Epistle, Gal. v. 25—vi. 10.
Gospel, Mat. vi. 24–34.

SIXTEENTH SUNDAY AFTER TRINITY.
Epistle, Ephes. iii. 13–21.
Gospel, Luke. vii. 11–17.

SEVENTEENTH SUNDAY AFTER TRINITY.
Epistle, Ephes. iv. 1–6.
Gospel, Luke xiv. 1–11.

EIGHTEENTH SUNDAY AFTER TRINITY.
Epistle, 1 Cor. i. 4–9.
Gospel, Mat. xxii. 34–46.

NINETEENTH SUNDAY AFTER TRINITY.
Epistle, Ephes. iv. 22–28.
Gospel, Mat. ix. 1–8.

TWENTIETH SUNDAY AFTER TRINITY.
Epistle, Ephes. v. 15–21.
Gospel, Mat. xxii. 1–14.

TWENTY-FIRST SUNDAY AFTER TRINITY.
Epistle, Ephes. vi. 10–17.
Gospel, John iv. 47–54.

TWENTY-SECOND SUNDAY AFTER TRINITY.
Epistle, Phil. i. 3–11.
Gospel, Mat. xviii. 23–35.

TWENTY-THIRD SUNDAY AFTER TRINITY.
Epistle, Phil. iii. 17–21.
Gospel, Mat. xxii. 15–22.

TWENTY-FOURTH SUNDAY AFTER TRINITY.
Epistle, Col. i. 9–14.
Gospel, Mat. ix. 18–26.

TWENTY-FIFTH SUNDAY AFTER TRINITY.
Epistle, 1 Thess. iv. 13–18.
Gospel, Mat. xxiv. 15–28.

TWENTY-SIXTH SUNDAY AFTER TRINITY.
Epistle, 2 Pet. iii. 3–14.
  Or, 2 Thess. i. 3–10.
Gospel, Mat. xxv. 31–46.

TWENTY-SEVENTH SUNDAY AFTER TRINITY.
Epistle, 1 Thess. v. 1–11.
  Or, Rom. iii. 21–28.
Gospel, Mat. xxv. 1–13.
  Or, Mat. xxiv. 37–51.
  Or, Mat. v. 1–2.

IX.
Scripture Lessons.

As the reading of the Scriptures is an important and essential part of public worship, it is in no wise to be neglected. The following selection of Scripture Lessons may be used at the Evening Service on the Lord's-day, and during the week.

I. FROM THE NEW TESTAMENT.

A. FROM THE GOSPELS.

Holy Seasons.

ADVENT.
Preparation for the birth of the Saviour.

I. Advent.	LUKE i. 1–25.	Annunciation of the birth of John.
II. Advent.	" i. 26–35.	Annunciation of the birth of our Lord.
III. Advent.	" i. 39–56.	Elizabeth and Mary.
IV. Advent.	" i. 67–80.	Birth of John the Baptist.

CHRISTMAS.

Christmas.	JOHN i. 1–14.	The Word became flesh.
II. Christmas.	" i. 15–18.	John testifies of him.
S. a. Christmas.	LUKE ii. 22–32.	Presentation of our Lord.
Sylvester Evening.	MAT. xvi. 1–12.	Signs of the times.
New-Year.	LUKE iv. 16–21.	The acceptable year of the Lord.

EPIPHANY.
Opening manifestations of the Messianic glory of our Lord.

S. a. New-Year.	MAT. iii. 1–12.	Ministry of John.
Epiphany.	" iii. 13–17.	Baptism of our Lord.
I. a. Epiphany.	JOHN i. 35–51.	The calling of the first disciples.
II. a. Epiphany.	" iii. 22–36.	John's conversation with his disples.
III. a. Epiphany.	MAT. iv. 12–17.	First preaching of our Lord.
IV. a. Epiphany.	JOHN iv. 4–24.	Jesus and the woman of Samaria.
V. a. Epiphany.	" iv. 25–42.	Jesus and the woman of Samaria.
VI. a. Epiphany.	MAT. xi. 25–30.	Invitation to the weary.
Septuagesima.	" xvi. 13–20.	Art thou the Christ?
Sexagesima.	" xvii. 1–9.	The Transfiguration.
Quinquagesima.	JOHN viii. 12–20.	The light of the world.

SCRIPTURE LESSONS.

LENT AND PASSION WEEK.

Resistance of unbelief to our Lord's glorious revelations.

I. Invocavit.	JOHN viii. 23–40.	Jesus foretells his sufferings.
II. Reminiscere.	" ix. 1–22.	Cure of one born blind.
III. Oculi.	" x. 23–38.	Opposition to Christ's teachings.
IV. Laetare.	" xi. 1–27.	Raising of Lazarus.
V. Judica.	" xi. 28–57.	Raising of Lazarus.
VI. Palmarum.	" xii. 1–19.	Anointing at Bethany and entrance into Jerusalem.
Thur. Pass. Week.	LUKE xxii. 7–23.	Institution of the Lord's Supper.
Good-Friday.	MAT. xxvii. 33–54.	Crucifixion.

EASTER.

Consideration of the resurrection of Jesus and his intercessory prayer in connection with it.

Easter Sunday.	MAT. xxviii. 1–10.	Account of the resurrection.
Easter Monday.	JOHN xx. 11–18.	Mary Magdalene.
Quasimod.	LUKE xxiv. 36–47.	It behooved Christ to suffer, and to rise.
Misericordias.	JOHN xxi. 1–19.	Jesus' appearance at the sea.
Jubilate.	" xvii. 1–8.	Glorify thou me, O Father.
Cantate.	" xvii. 9–19.	Intercessions for the disciples.
Rogate.	" xvii. 20–26.	Intercessions for future believers.

ASCENSION.

Ascension.	LUKE xxiv. 44–53.	Our Lord's ascension.
Exaudi.	JOHN xiv. 1–14.	I am the way.

PENTECOST.

Whitsunday.	JOHN xiv. 15–21.	He shall give you another Comforter.
Whitmonday.	" xv. 1–8	I am the true vine.
Trinity Sunday.	MAT. xxviii. 18-20.	Baptism in the name of the Triune God.

TRINITY SUNDAYS.

The discourses of our Lord, ending with his teachings concerning the final consummation.

I. a. Trinity.	MAT. v. 1–12.	The beatitudes.
II. a. Trinity.	" v. 13–19.	The salt of the earth.
III. a. Trinity.	" v. 27–42.	Pluck it out.
IV. a. Trinity.	" v. 43–48.	Love your enemies.
V. a. Trinity.	" vi. 1–15.	Of alms-giving and prayer.
VI. a. Trinity.	" vi. 16–23.	Of the true treasure and light.
VII. a. Trinity.	" vii. 1–14.	Entrance at the strait gate.
VIII. a. Trinity.	" vii. 24–29.	The house on the rock and that on the sand.
IX. a. Trinity.	JOHN v. 19–29.	Faith in Christ true life.
X. a. Trinity.	" v. 30–36.	Jesus' works witness of him.
XI. a. Trinity.	" v. 37–47.	The scriptures witness of him.

SCRIPTURE LESSONS. 147

XII. a. Trinity.	JOHN vi. 30–51.	Jesus the bread of life.
XIII. a. Trinity.	MARK iv. 26–34.	Parables of the seed.
XIV. a. Trinity.	LUKE xii. 32–38.	Fear not, little flock.
XV. a. Trinity.	" xiii. 1–9,	The fruitless fig-tree.
XVI. a. Trinity.	MAT. xiii. 44–52.	Of the treasure, the pearl and the net.
XVII. a. Trinity.	LUKE xv. 11–32.	The prodigal son.
XVIII. a. Trinity.	MARK x. 1–12.	Of divorce.
XIX. a. Trinity.	MAT. xv. 1–11.	Traditions of men.
XX. a. Trinity.	" xix. 16–26.	The rich young man.
XXI. a. Trinity.	" xxi. 33–44.	The wicked husbandmen.
XXII. a. Trinity.	JOHN xv. 18–25.	The hatred of the world.
XXIII. a. Trinity.	MARK xii. 18–27.	The Sadducees confuted.
XXIV. a. Trinity.	" xiii. 1–13.	Destruction of Jerusalem and the end of the world.
XXV. a. Trinity.	LUKE xvii. 20–37.	The coming of the Son of man.
XXVI. a. Trinity.	MAT. xxv. 14–30.	Parable of the talents.
XXVII. a. Trin.	LUKE xiii. 23–30.	Strive to enter in at the strait gate.
Harvest festival.	" xii. 13–21.	The rich man's barn.
Reformation.	JOHN ii. 13–17.	Jesus purgeth the temple.
Thanksgiving.	PSALM cxlvi.	Praise the Lord, O my soul.
Humiliation.	" cxliii.	O Lord, hear my prayer.

B. FROM THE OTHER BOOKS OF THE NEW TESTAMENT.

ADVENT.

Preparation for the coming of Christ and its influence.

I. Advent.	COL. i. 16–23.	God's eternal purpose.
II. Advent.	ROMANS i. 16–25.	Condition of the heathen without Christ.
III. Advent.	" ii. 1–12.	Israel also under condemnation.
IV. Advent.	HEB. xii. 15–25.	Sinai and Zion.

CHRISTMAS.

Christmas.	HEBREWS i. 1–12.	Christ the Son of God.
II. Christmas.	1 JOHN iv. 7–16.	God's love manifest in Christ.
S. a. Christmas.	HEBREWS iii. 1–6.	Christ more worthy than Moses.
Sylvester Even.	1 PETER i. 22–25.	All flesh is as grass.
New-Year.	" ii. 1–10.	Lay aside all malice.

EPIPHANY.

Exposition of the growth of faith.

S. a. New-Year.	ROM. vii. 7–25.	Knowledge of sin.
Epiphany.	" iii. 23–31.	The heathen also justified through Christ.
I. a. Epiphany.	EPH. ii. 11–22.	Aforetime heathens, now in Christ.
II. a. Epiphany.	ROM. iv. 16–25.	The faith of Abraham.
III. a. Epiphany.	" v. 1–5.	Peace with God through faith.
IV. a. Epiphany.	" viii. 1–11.	Being spiritually minded.

V. a. Epiphany.	1 Cor. ii. 1–10.	The wisdom of the perfect.
VI. a. Epiphany.	James iii. 13–18.	Who is wise among you?
Septuagesima.	2 Cor. viii. 1–9.	Liberality to poor brethren.
Sexagesima.	Rom. xiv. 13–19.	Love and mutual improvement.
Quinquagesima.	" x. 8–18.	Confession of faith.

LENT AND PASSION WEEK.

The suffering Christ, and the suffering of believers.

Invocavit.	Hebrew xii. 1–6.	Looking unto Jesus.
Reminiscere.	Rom. viii. 28–39.	All things for good to believers.
Oculi.	2 Cor. iv. 7–14.	The death and life of Christ manifest in us.
Laetare.	" v. 14–21.	One died for all.
Judica.	1 Peter i. 13–21.	Redeemed not with silver and gold.
Palmarum.	Heb. x. 19–27.	Entrance into the holiest.
Thur. Pass. Week.	1 Cor. x. 16–22.	The Lord's Supper the communion of Christ.
Good-Friday.	Rev. v. 1–14.	Praise of the Lamb that is slain.

EASTER.

The resurrection of Christ, his exaltation in general.

Easter Sunday.	1 Cor. xv. 12–28.	Now is Christ risen.
Easter Monday.	" xv. 35–49.	How shall the dead rise?
Quasimod.	" xv. 50–58.	Death is swallowed up in victory.
Misericordias.	1 John. i. 1–7.	Walk in light.
Jubilate.	" ii. 12–17.	Your sins are forgiven you.
Cantate.	" iii. 1–11.	Behold what manner of love.
Rogate.	" v. 12–21.	He that hath the Son hath life.

ASCENSION.

Ascension.	Eph. iv. 7–16.	He has ascended and become the Head.
Exaudi.	Acts. i. 12–26.	The Apostles after the Lord's ascension.

PENTECOST.

Whitsunday.	Acts. ii. 14–41.	Peter's first preaching and its results.
Whitmonday.	Rom. x. 11–17.	How beautiful the feet of them that preach peace.
Trinity Sunday.	Eph. i. 3–14.	Father, Son, and Holy Ghost.

TRINITY SUNDAYS.

The work established by Jesus, with a glance at his second coming.

I. a. Trinity.	Acts. ii. 42–47.	Life of the first congregation.
II. a. Trinity.	" iii. 1–10.	Healing of the lame man at the temple.
III. a. Trinity.	" iii. 11–26.	Peter's sermon after the miracle.
IV. a. Trinity.	" iv. 1–22.	Peter and John before the council.
V. a. Trinity.	" iv. 23–31.	The church gives thanks to God.

SCRIPTURE LESSONS. 149

VI. a. Trinity.	ACTS iv. 32, v. 11.	Ananias and Sapphira.
VII. a. Trinity.	" v. 12–42.	Imprisonment of the Apostles.
VIII. a. Trinity.	" vi. 1–7.	Election of Deacons.
IX. a. Trinity.	" vii. 51–59.	Martyrdom of Stephen.
X. a. Trinity.	" viii. 9–25.	Simon the sorcerer.
XI. a. Trinity.	" viii. 26–39.	The Ethiopian eunuch.
XII. a. Trinity.	" ix. 1–22.	Conversion of Paul.
XIII. a. Trinity.	" x. 21–33. xi. 1–18.	Conversion of Cornelius and Peter's defence.
XIV. a. Trinity.	" xiv. 1–20.	Paul at Iconium.
XV. a. Trinity.	" xvi. 13–40.	Paul at Philippi.
XVI. a. Trinity.	" xvii. 15–34,	Paul at Athens,
XVII. a. Trinity.	" xviii. 1–11.	Paul at Corinth.
XVIII. a. Trinity.	" xix. 1–11.	Paul at Ephesus.
XIX. a. Trinity.	" xx. 17–38.	Departure from Miletus.
XX. a. Trinity.	" xxiv. 10–27.	Paul before Felix and Drusilla.
XXI. a. Trinity.	" xxvi. 1–29.	Paul before Festus and Agrippa.
XXII. a. Trinity.	" xxviii. 1-10, 16–31.	Paul at Melita and Rome.
XXIII. a. Trinity.	REV. ii. 1–11.	Messages to the churches of Ephesus and Smyrna.
XXIV. a. Trinity.	" iii. 1–22.	Messages to Sardis, Philadelphia and Laodicea.
XXV. a. Trinity.	" vii. 9–17.	The great multitude of the redeemed.
XXVI. a. Trinity.	" xx. 11–15.	The judgment.
XXVII. a. Trin.	" xxii. 6–21.	Behold I come quickly.
Harvest festival.	1 TIM. vi. 6–10.	Great gain.
Reformation.	GAL. ii. 16–21.	The mode of justification.
Thanksgiving.	PSALM cxlv.	The greatness and goodness of God.
Humiliation.	PSALM cxxx.	Out of the depths.

II. FROM THE OLD TESTAMENT.

A. SELECTIONS CHIEFLY HISTORICAL.

ADVENT.

Bright stars in the prophetic night of the time before Christ.

I. Advent.	GEN. iii. 1–15.	The first promise after the fall.
II. Advent.	JER. xxxi. 31–36.	The new covenant.
III. Advent.	ISA. lv. 3–13.	An everlasting covenant.
IV. Advent.	PSALM c.	Make a joyful noise to the Lord.

CHRISTMAS.

Christmas.	ISAIAH ix. 2–7.	Unto us a child is born.
II. Christmas.	" xi. 1–5.	The rod of the stem of Jesse.
S. a. Christmas.	" xii. 1–6.	A joyful thanksgiving.
" "	PSALM cii. 25–29.	Take us not away O God.
Sylvester Evening.	" xc.	O Lord thou art our dwelling place.
New-Year.	" cxi.	Praise God for his wonderful works.

13*

SCRIPTURE LESSONS.

EPIPHANY.

Light from God in the times of the Patriarchs.

S. a. New-Year.	GEN. xi. 1-9.	The tower of Babel.
Epiphany.	" xii. 1-4. xiii. 5-11.	Calling of Abraham.
I. a. Epiphany.	" xiv. 8-20.	Melchizedek's blessing.
II. a. Epiphany.	" xv. 1-17.	Covenant with Abraham.
III. a. Epiphany.	" xviii. 20-33.	Abraham's intercessions for Sodom.
IV. a. Epiphany.	" xxii. 1-19.	The offering of Isaac.
V. a. Epiphany.	" xxiv. 34-51.	Isaac's marriage to Rebecca.
VI. a. Epiphany.	" xxviii. 10-22	Jacob's ladder at Bethel.
Septuages.	" xli. 28-43.	Joseph's advancement.
Sexages.	" xlix. 1-33.	Jacob takes leave of his sons.
Quinquag.	" l. 15-22.	Joseph nobly pardons his brethren.

LENT AND PASSION WEEK.

Oppression of the children of Israel in Egypt, and God's succour.

Invocavit.	Ex. i. 3-22.	Pharaoh's oppressions.
Reminiscere.	" ii. 1-10.	Preservation of Moses.
Oculi.	" ii. 11-15.	Moses' flight into Midian.
Laetare.	" iii. 1-14.	The call of Moses.
Judica.	" v. 1-21.	Continued oppressions of the people.
Palmarum.	" v. 22. vi. 9.	Promise of deliverance.
Thur. Pass. Week.	PSALM xxiii.	Thou preparest a table before us.
Good-Friday.	Ex. xii. 1-14.	The blood of the Paschal Lamb.

EASTER.

Deliverance of the children of Israel and gracious guidance of them through the wilderness.

Easter Sunday.	JOB xix. 22-27.	I know that my Redeemer liveth.
Easter Monday.	Ps. cxviii. 14-29.	A song of victory.
Quasimod.	Ex. xv. 1-21.	Song of triumph at the Red Sea.
Misericord.	" xv. 22-26.	Marah. The Lord our physician.
Jubilate.	" xvi. 1-15.	Quails and manna.
Cantate.	" xvii. 1-16.	Water from the rock and the victory.
Rogate.	PSALM cxvi.	The Lord heareth.

ASCENSION.

Ascension.	GEN. v. 21-24.	The translation of Enoch.
Exaudi.	Ex. xix. 3-8.	Israel set apart as a peculiar people.

PENTECOST.

Whitsunday.	JOEL ii. 21. iii. 1.	I will pour out my Spirit.
Whitmonday.	PSALM cxxii.	The glory of Jerusalem.
Trinity Sunday.	NUM. vi. 22-27.	The Old Testament Benediction.

SCRIPTURE LESSONS. 151

TRINITY SUNDAYS.

Continuation of the history of the Kingdom of God in Israel to the return from the Babylonian captivity.

I. a. Trinity.	Ex. xxxiv. 1–10.	The Lord God, merciful and gracious.
II. a. Trinity.	Num. xxi. 4–9.	The brazen serpent.
III. a. Trinity.	" xxiii. 7–12.	Balaam's blessing.
IV. a. Trinity.	Josh. xxiv. 14–28.	I and my house.
V. a. Trinity.	Judges ii. 1–12.	Wickedness of Israel after Joshua's death.
VI. a. Trinity.	Ruth i. 1–17.	Ruth's steadfastness.
VII. a. Trinity.	1 Sam. iii. 1–18.	God calleth Samuel.
VIII. a. Trinity.	" x. 17–27.	Election of Saul.
IX. a. Trinity.	" xv. 16–23.	Saul's disobedience.
X. a. Trinity.	" xxiv. 2–23.	David's generosity toward Saul.
XI. a. Trinity.	2 Sam. vii. 1–16.	Promises for the erection of the temple.
XII. a. Trinity.	" vii. 17–29.	David's thanksgiving therefor.
XIII. a. Trinity.	" xii. 1–10.	Nathan's reproof of David.
XIV. a. Trinity.	" xxiii. 1–7.	David's last words.
XV. a. Trinity.	1 Kings iii. 5–15.	Solomon's prayer for wisdom.
XVI. a. Trinity.	2 Chr. vii. 12–22.	God's appearance to Solomon.
XVII. a. Trinity.	" xiii. 3–18.	Israel's defection and danger.
XVIII. a. Trinity.	1 Kin. xviii. 21–40	Elijah and Baal's Prophets.
XIX. a. Trinity.	" xix. 4–18.	Elijah weary of life is consoled.
XX. a. Trinity.	2 Kings v. 1–14.	Elisha heals Naaman.
XXI. a. Trinity.	Jon. iii. 1—iv. 11.	Jonah preaches repentance at Nineveh.
XXII. a. Trinity.	2 Ch. xxxii. 1–21.	Hezekiah delivered from Sennacherib.
XXIII. a. Trinity.	" xxxiv. 14-28.	The finding of the law under Josiah.
XXIV. a. Trinity.	" xxxvi. 11-21.	The removal to Babylon.
XXV. a. Trinity.	Dan. ii. 31–48.	The dream of the eternal Kingdom.
XXVI. a. Trinity.	Ezra iii. 10–13.	The foundation of the new temple.
XXVII. a. Trin.	Mal. iii. 1–5.	The coming of the Judge.
Harvest Festival.	Deut. xxvi. 1–11.	Prayer of thanks for the harvest.
Reformation.	2 Ch. xxxiv. 29-33	Josiah's renewal of the covenant.
Thanksgiving.	Psalm xcv. 1–8.	Let us sing unto the Lord.
Humiliation.	" lxxxv.	Show us thy mercy, O Lord.

B. PROPHETIC AND POETIC SELECTIONS.

ADVENT.

I. Advent.	Psalm xl.	Lo, I come, it is written of me.
II. Advent.	Prov. viii. 22–31.	True wisdom.
	Psalm viii.	What is man?
III. Advent.	Isaiah xl. 1–9.	The voice in the wilderness.
IV. Advent.	Psalm xxiv.	Lift up your heads, O ye gates.

SCRIPTURE LESSONS.

CHRISTMAS.

Christmas.	Micah v. 1-3.	Thou, Bethlehem Ephratah.
II. Christmas.	Psalm cxlviii.	Praise ye the Lord.
S. a. Christmas.	" ii.	Kiss the Son.
Sylvester Evening.	" cxxix.	Lord, thou hast searched me.
New-Year.	Isaiah xl. 26-31.	They that wait upon the Lord.
"	Psalm cxxi.	I will lift up mine eyes.

EPIPHANY.

Attendance upon the Lord on his way as Prophet.

S. a. New-Year.	1 Sam. ii. 1-10.	He will exalt the horn of his anointed.
Epiphany.	Isaiah ii. 1-5.	Out of Zion shall go forth the law.
"	" xlii. 1-12.	He shall bring judgment to the Gentiles.
I. a. Epiphany.	Deu. xviii. 15-19.	A Prophet like unto Moses.
"	Psalm i.	The way of the godly and of the ungodly.
II. a. Epiphany.	Isaiah lxi. 1-6.	The Spirit of the Lord is upon me.
III. a. Epiphany.	Amos iii. 1-8.	The secrets of the Lord revealed to the Prophets.
IV. a. Epiphany.	Micah vi. 1-8.	What service God roquireth.
V. a. Epiphany.	" vii. 14-20.	He will do wonders as aforetime.
VI. a. Epiphany.	Haggai ii. 2-10.	The glory of the second temple.
Septuages.	Mal. ii. 4-10.	The unfaithful servants reproved.
Sexages.	Amos viii. 1-14.	God's word removed from the wicked.
Quinquag.	Hab. ii. 1-14.	The earth shall be full of the knowledge of the Lord.

LENT AND PASSION WEEK.

Attendance upon the Lord on his way as the Lamb of God.

Invocavit.	Isaiah l. 4-10.	Christ's patient suffering.
Reminiscere.	Psalm li.	Penitential prayer of the sinner.
Oculi.	" xxii.	Prophecy of the suffering Saviour.
Laetare.	Isa. lxiv. 1-12.	The church's prayer of penitence.
Judica.	Job xxxiii. 13-30.	Our sufferings in God's hands.
Palmarum.	Zech. ix. 8-12.	Zion, the King of peace cometh to thee.
Thur. Pass. Week.	Psalm xxv.	Unto thee O Lord, do I lift up my soul.
Good-Friday.	Isa. lii. 13. liii. 12.	The suffering Saviour.

EASTER.

The victory over death and the great and gracious promises of God to his people.

Easter Sunday.	Isa. xxv. 1-8.	He will swallow up death in victory.
Easter Monday.	Eze. xxxvii. 1-14.	Vision of the resurrection of the dead.
Quasimod.	Isaiah iv. 2-6.	The blessings of Christ's kingdom.
Misericord.	Eze. xxxiv. 11-16.	God's providence over his flock.
Jubilate.	Hosea ii. 18-23.	I will betroth thee unto me forever.

SCRIPTURE LESSONS. 153

Cantate.	Isa. xlix. 8–15.	The Lord will not forget his people.
Rogate.	Psalm lxxxvi.	Give ear, O Lord, unto my prayer.

ASCENSION.

Ascension.	Psalm cx.	Sit thou at my right hand.
Exaudi.	Isa. xxxii. 14–20.	A land only prosperous when the Spirit is poured out.

PENTECOST.

Whitsunday.	Joel ii. 28–32.	I will pour out my Spirit upon all flesh.
Whitmonday.	Eze. xxxvi. 25-28.	A new heart will I give you.
Trinity Sunday.	Isaiah vi. 1–8.	Holy, holy, holy is the Lord of Hosts.

TRINITY SUNDAYS.

Concerning God, the christian life, and the judgment.

I. a. Trinity.	Psalm lxii.	In God is my salvation.
II. a. Trinity.	Job xxxvi. 26. xxxvii. 13.	The praise of God by nature.
III. a. Trinity.	Eze. xviii. 20–24.	God is just.
IV. a. Trinity.	Psalm ciii.	God is gracious.
V. a. Trinity.	Lam. iii. 22–40.	God is long-suffering.
VI. a. Trinity.	Psalm xci.	God is a defence to the godly.
VII. a. Trinity.	Eccles. iii. 1–17.	To everything there is a time.
VIII. a. Trinity.	Ps. cxix. 105–112.	Thy word is a lamp unto my feet.
IX. a. Trinity.	" liii.	The fool knoweth him not.
X. a. Trinity.	Jer. viii. 4–9.	What wisdom is in them who reject the word of the Lord?
XI. a. Trinity.	Eze. xiii. 9–16.	False Prophets.
XII. a. Trinity.	Prov. ix. 1–18.	The call of wisdom, and of folly.
XIII. a. Trinity.	Job xxxviii. 1–11.	God brings to nought man's pride.
XIV. a. Trinity.	Prov. iii. 1–16.	The nature and results of wisdom.
XV. a. Trinity.	Deut. vi. 4–13.	Love to the one God.
XVI. a. Trinity.	Jer. xvii. 5–10.	Trust in God.
XVII. a. Trinity.	Lev. xix. 9–18.	Brotherly kindness.
XVIII. a. Trinity.	Deut. xxi. 18–21.	Obedience to parents.
XIX. a. Trinity.	" xxiv. 17-22.	Charity toward widows and orphans.
XX. a. Trinity.	Prov. vi. 6–11.	Industry.
XXI. a. Trinity.	" xxiii. 19-35.	Warning against riotous living.
XXII. a. Trinity.	" xxiv. 13-22.	Wise preparation for the future.
XXIII. a. Trinity.	Ec. xi. 9. xii. 14.	Joy of a life spent in the fear of God.
XXIV. a. Trinity.	Prov. xxx. 1–14.	Of an unbelieving generation.
XXV. a. Trinity.	Mal. iii. 13. iv. 6.	The day of judgment.
XXVI. a. Trinity.	Deu. xxxii. 21-43.	Song of Moses: Judgment and redemption.
XXVII. a. Trin.	Psalm xcii.	It is good to give thanks unto the Lord.
Harvest Festival.	" lxv.	Thou visitest the earth.
Reformation.	" xlvi. or cxix. 29–43.	God is our refuge.
Thanksgiving.	Ps. lxxviii. 1–7.	God's benefits to his people.
Humiliation.	Isaiah i. 16–18.	Wash ye, make you clean.

PART SECOND.

I.
The Order of Holy Baptism.

The Baptism of Infants.

BAPTISM *should be administered in the Church, in the presence of the congregation; it may, however, be administered privately. Parents may present their child for Baptism; or they may appoint others as Sponsors. The Minister shall see that the Sponsors are members of the Church, and do not live in open sin. Should the Parents not be members of a christian congregation, he shall admonish them to become such. The Minister shall enter the names of the Parents, of the Child, and of the Sponsors, with the date of its birth and Baptism, in the Church Record. At the Baptism the following order shall be observed: The Parents or Sponsors, shall present the Child at the Font, and the Minister shall say:*

DEARLY Beloved, forasmuch as all men are conceived and born in sin; and our Saviour Christ saith, Except a man be born again of water and of the Spirit, he cannot enter into the kingdom of God; I beseech you to call upon God the Father, through our Lord Jesus Christ, that of his goodness and mercy, he would receive this child, by baptism, into the Church of the Redeemer, and make it a living member of the same. And forasmuch as this child promises, by you its sureties, to renounce the devil and all his works, to believe in God and to serve him; you must remember that it is your bounden duty to see that it be taught, so soon as it shall be able to learn, what a solemn promise you have made in its name. And that it may know these things the better, you should admonish it to give due heed to the instruction given in Church and at school, and to all those things which a christian ought to know and believe to his soul's salvation; and that thus this child may be virtuously brought up to lead a godly and a christian life; remembering always that Baptism doth represent unto us our profession; which is, to follow the example of our Saviour Christ, and to be made like unto him. For as many of us as have been baptized, have put on Christ, that like as he died for us and rose again, so should we die daily unto sin and rise again unto righteousness.

Let us pray :

ALMIGHTY and everlasting God, the Father of our Lord Jesus Christ; we call upon thee for this child, and beseech thee to bestow upon it the gift of thy Baptism and thine everlasting grace by the washing of regeneration. Receive it, O Lord, as thou hast promised by thy well-beloved Son, saying : Ask, and it shall be given you; seek, and ye shall find; knock, and it shall be opened unto you. So give now unto us who ask; let us who seek, find; open the gate unto us who knock; that this child may enjoy the everlasting benediction of thy heavenly washing, and may come to the eternal kingdom which thou hast promised by Christ our Lord. *Amen.*

HEAR the words of the Gospel, written by St. Mark, in the tenth chapter, at the thirteenth verse.

THEY brought young children to Jesus, that he should touch them; and his disciples rebuked those that brought them. But when Jesus saw it, he was much displeased, and said unto them, Suffer the little children to come unto me, and forbid them not: for of such is the kingdom of God. Verily I say unto you, Whosoever shall not receive the kingdom of God as a little child, he shall not enter therein. And he took them up in his arms, put his hands upon them, and blessed them.

Then the Minister, laying his right hand on the head of the Child, shall pray :

OUR Father, who art in heaven; Hallowed be thy name; Thy kingdom come; Thy will be done on earth, as it is in heaven; Give us this day our daily bread; And forgive us our trespasses, as we forgive those who trespass against us; And lead us not into temptation; But deliver us from evil; For thine is the kingdom, and the power, and the glory, for ever and ever. *Amen.*

The Minister shall then demand of the Parents or Sponsors, as follows:

DO you, in the name of this child, renounce the devil, and all his works, and all his ways? Then answer, *Yes.*

Do you believe in God the Father Almighty, Maker of heaven and earth?

And in Jesus Christ his only Son, our Lord; Who was conceived by the Holy Ghost, Born of the Virgin Mary; Suffered under Pontius Pilate, Was crucified, dead, and buried; He descended into hell; The third day he rose again from the dead; He ascended into heaven, And sitteth on the right hand of God the Father Almighty; From thence he shall come to judge the quick and the dead?

Do you believe in the Holy Ghost; The holy Christian Church, the Communion of Saints; The forgiveness of sins; The Resurrection of the body; And the life everlasting? Then answer, *Yes.*

Do you desire that this child should be baptized in this Faith, and do you promise to use your endeavors that it may be trained up in the religion of Christ? Then answer, *Yes.*

Baptism is not simply water, but it is the water comprehended in God's command, and connected with God's word.

Then shall the Minister ask:

How shall the child be named?

Then shall he baptize it, saying:

N. I baptize thee in the name of the Father, and of the Son, and of the Holy Ghost. *Amen.*

A suitable verse may then be sung. Then shall the Minister say the following:

WE yield thee hearty thanks, most merciful Father, that in holy Baptism thou hast received and adopted this child as thine own, regenerated it of water and of the Spirit, and incorporated it into thy holy Church. And we humbly beseech thee to grant, that it being dead unto sin, may live unto righteousness. May it be buried with Christ, by Baptism, into his death; that as it is made partaker of the death of thy dear Son, it may also be partaker of his glorious resurrection; so that finally, with the residue of thy holy Church, it may be an heir of thine everlasting kingdom, through Jesus Christ, our Lord and Saviour. *Amen.*

Peace be with you. *Amen.*

The Baptism of Adults.

The Minister standing before the altar shall say:

IN the name of the Father, and of the Son, and of the Holy Ghost. *Amen.*

DEARLY Beloved, we learn from the word of God, and from the testimony of our own lives, that all men are conceived and born in sin, and that we must all assuredly perish, except our blessed Lord and Saviour, the only begotten Son of God, deliver us from our sins and guilt. Inasmuch as *this person*, who now desires to be baptized, *is* of like sinful and depraved nature, and our Lord Jesus Christ has borne in his own body the sins of the whole world, and has redeemed and delivered us from death and from everlasting damnation; I beseech you to call upon God, through our Lord Christ, that of his goodness and mercy, he would receive *this person*, truly repenting and coming unto him by faith, into the kingdom of his grace, and bestow upon *him* everlasting life; confidently believing that he will accept your offering and intercession of love, and will assuredly hear your prayer.

Let us pray.

ALMIGHTY and everlasting God, the Father of our Lord Jesus Christ, the aid of all who need, the helper of all who flee to thee for succour, the life of those who believe, and the resurrection of the dead; we call upon thee for *this person* who desires the gift of thy Baptism, and thine everlasting grace, by spiritual regeneration. Receive *him*, O Lord, as thou hast promised by thy well-beloved Son, saying: Ask, and it shall be given you; seek, and ye shall find; knock, and it shall be opened unto you. So give now unto *him* who asketh; let *him* who seeketh, find; open the gate unto *him* who knocketh; that *this person* may enjoy the everlasting benediction of thy heavenly washing, and may come to the eternal kingdom which thou hast promised by Christ our Lord.

Then shall the Congregation say:

Amen.

Hear the words of our Lord. (Mat. xxviii. 18–20.)

ALL power is given unto me in heaven and in earth. Go ye therefore, and teach all nations, baptizing them in the name of the Father, and of the Son, and of the Holy Ghost; teaching them to observe all things whatsoever I have commanded you; and lo, I am with you alway, even unto the end of the world.

In like manner he says: (Mark xvi. 16,) He that

believeth and is baptized, shall be saved; but he that believeth not shall be damned.

In accordance with this command of our Lord Jesus, *this person* has been instructed in the saving doctrines of the gospel, and now desires, by holy Baptism to be incorporated into the Church of Christ. Forasmuch then as we do not doubt that it is right that *his* desire should be granted, let us pray that God would bestow upon *him* everlasting life.

OUR Father, who art in heaven; Hallowed be thy name; Thy kingdom come; Thy will be done on earth, as it is in heaven; Give us this day our daily bread; And forgive us our trespasses, as we forgive those who trespass against us; And lead us not into temptation; But deliver us from evil; For thine is the kingdom, and the power, and the glory, for ever and ever.

Then shall the Congregation with the Person to be baptized say:

Amen.

Then shall the Minister say to the Person to be baptized:

THE Lord preserve thy going out and thy coming in, from this time forth, and even for evermore.

The Minister shall then demand of the Person to be baptized as follows:

Do you renounce the devil, and all his works, and all his ways?

Answer.

Yes, I renounce.

Minister.

Do you believe in God the Father Almighty, Maker of heaven and earth?

And in Jesus Christ his only Son, our Lord; Who was conceived by the Holy Ghost, Born of the Virgin Mary; Suffered under Pontius Pilate, Was crucified, dead, and buried; He descended into hell; The third day he rose again from the dead; He ascended into heaven, And sitteth on the right hand of God the

Father Almighty; From thence he shall come to judge the quick and the dead? Do you believe in the Holy Ghost; The holy Christian Church, the Communion of Saints; The forgiveness of sins; The Resurrection of the body; And the life everlasting?

Answer.

Yes, I believe.

Minister.

Do you sincerely desire to be baptized in this Faith, and to make your covenant with God?

Answer.

Yes, that is my sincere desire.

Minister.

O LORD God, Father, Son, and Holy Ghost; thou hearest the solemn vows of *this* thy *servant*. Receive *him* then into the covenant of thy grace, and let *him* have part in all the benefits secured unto us through Jesus Christ our Lord.

Then shall the Person to be baptized kneel down, and the Minister, pouring water on his head three times, shall say:

N. I baptize thee, in the name of the Father, and of the Son, and of the Holy Ghost.

Then laying his hand upon his head he shall say:

ALMIGHTY God, the Father of our Lord Jesus Christ, who hath begotten thee again of water and of the Holy Ghost, and forgiven thee all thy sins, strengthen and keep thee by his grace unto life eternal. Peace be with thee.

Then shall the Congregation say:

Amen.

The Person baptized now standing up, the Minister shall say:

DEARLY Beloved in Christ Jesus, seeing that it has pleased a merciful God to receive unto himself, in holy Baptism, *this* our *Brother*, let us render praise and thanksgiving unto him, and with one accord beseech him, that he would continue his fatherly blessing to *him*, and to us, unto the end of our lives.

Let us pray :

ALMIGHTY and most merciful God and Father, we yield thee most hearty thanks that thou dost graciously preserve and extend thy Church, and that thou hast caused *this* thy *servant* to be born again in holy Baptism, to be incorporated into thy dear Son our Lord and only Saviour, and to become thy child and an heir of thy heavenly grace. We do most humbly beseech thee that thou wouldst keep *him*, and all of us who have been baptized, in steadfast continuance in thy grace, so that here on earth we may lead truly godly lives, according to thy good-pleasure and to the praise and glory of thy holy name, and in the end may receive the promised inheritance in heaven, through Jesus Christ our Lord, who ever liveth and reigneth with thee and the Holy Ghost, world without end. *Amen.*

THEREFORE, dear *Brother*, let your conversation be as it becometh the gospel of Christ.—(Phil. i. 27.) Show forth the praises of him who hath called you out of darkness into his marvellous light.—(1 Pet. ii. 9.) Be not ashamed of the gospel of Christ: for it is the power of God unto salvation to every one that believeth.—(Rom. i. 16.) Fight the good fight of faith, lay hold on eternal life, whereunto thou art also called, and hast professed a good profession before many witnesses.—(1 Tim. vi. 12.)

And the very God of peace sanctify you wholly: and I pray God your whole spirit and soul and body be preserved blameless unto the coming of our Lord Jesus Christ. Faithful is he that calleth you, who also will do it. *Amen.*

II.

The Order of Confirmation.

CONFIRMATION *should take place in the Church, in the presence of the congregation. Only when by reason of sickness, or other causes, this is impossible, can it be administered privately.*

The Minister, standing before the Altar, shall say :

THE Lord be with you!

The Congregation shall answer :—

And with thy spirit!

Minister.

Let the beauty of the Lord our God be upon us; and establish thou the work of our hands upon us!

Congregation.

Yea the work of our hands establish thou it!

Minister.

DEARLY beloved in the Lord! You see here present those who in holy Baptism were received by our Lord Jesus Christ and made members of his holy Church. In accordance with our Lord's command, they have been instructed in the word of God, and led to the knowledge of his will, and of his gracious gospel; and they now desire to be confirmed. It is their hearty wish to be admitted to the enjoyment of all those blessings which the Lord bestows upon his Church, and by partaking of his holy supper to be brought into the most intimate union with our Lord and Saviour Jesus Christ. They desire publicly to confess their Christian Faith, and for themselves to renew and ratify the promises made for them by their Sponsors in holy Baptism. Let us therefore beseech Almighty God, our heavenly Father, in the name of our Lord Jesus Christ; that he would confirm them, so strengthening them by the grace of his Holy Spirit, that they may be kept in the true faith, and in purity and holiness of life, steadfast unto the end.

O LORD God, most merciful Father, who dost receive children into thy kingdom, and dost esteem their souls precious in thy sight; we beseech thee, of thy great goodness; that thou wouldst, by thy Holy Spirit, so bless and govern these persons consecrated to thee in holy Baptism, that they may make a good confession of thy name, that they may ever live in the communion of thy Church, in true faith and obedience to thy gospel, and that they may continue steadfast in the covenant of thy grace unto the end; through Jesus Christ, thy dear Son, our Lord. *Amen.*

The Minister shall then demand of the Catechumens as follows:

1. I ask you, in the presence of the Omniscient God, and of this Congregation;

Is it your sincere purpose now solemnly to ratify your baptismal covenant, and to renounce the dominion of the devil, of the world, and of sin? Then answer:

Yes, it is our sincere purpose.

2. Do you believe in the Triune God, Father, Son, and Holy Ghost; and are you resolved to live in fellowship with him, and to attain to the blessed liberty of the true followers of Christ. Then answer:

Yes, we believe.

3. Will you remain faithful to the doctrines of our Lord Jesus, according to the confession of our Evangelical Lutheran Church, and will you render a conscientious obedience thereto until death? Then answer:

Yes, we will, by the help of God.

The Catechumens shall then kneel, and the Minister laying his right hand on the head of each, shall say one of the following sentences:

Receive the Holy Spirit, to protect and defend you against all evil, to strengthen and help you in all good; from the merciful hand of the Father, and of the Son, and of the Holy Ghost. Amen.

Thou Shepherd and Bishop of souls, look in mercy upon this thy servant, and let *him* never be plucked out of thy hand; keep *him* in thy fold unto the end of *his* days, according to thy gracious promise. Amen.

The Father of mercies, and the God of all consolation, grant you, for Christ's sake, his Holy Spirit, guidance and strength to do his will, patience and courage in time of suffering, and the blessed hope of everlasting life. Amen.

The God of all grace, who hath called us unto his eternal glory by Christ Jesus, make you perfect, stablish, strengthen, settle you, and keep you through faith unto life everlasting.

The very God of peace sanctify you wholly, that your whole spirit, and soul, and body, may be preserved blameless unto the coming of our Lord Jesus Christ.

May God, which hath begun a good work in you, perform it until the day of Jesus Christ.

Our heavenly Father increase and confirm within you, for Jesus Christ's sake, the gifts of his Holy Spirit; that so you may grow in faith, and in the power of godliness, in patience under suffering, and in the blessed hope of everlasting life.

May God, the Father of our Lord Jesus Christ, give unto you his Holy Spirit, to guide you into all truth, to defend you against all temptations, to strengthen you unto every good work, and to bring you at last unto his eternal joy.

Our Lord Jesus Christ, and God, even our Father, which hath loved us, and hath given us everlasting consolation, and good hope through grace, comfort and strengthen your heart to be faithful unto death, that you may receive the crown of life.

The God of peace make you perfect in every good work, to do his will, working in you that which is well-pleasing in his sight, through Jesus Christ; to whom be glory for ever and ever.

Grace be unto you, that you may fight the good fight of faith, and lay hold on eternal life, whereunto thou art also called, and hast professed a good profession before many witnesses.

The love of Christ so constrain you that you may live henceforth not unto yourself, but unto him which died for you and rose again.

Receive the Holy Spirit, to protect and defend you against all evil, to strengthen and help you unto all good, that you may glorify God in your body, and in your spirit, which are God's.

All then rising, the Minister shall give to each the right hand of fellowship, saying:

UPON the voluntary profession and promises which you have now made, I hereby acknowledge and declare you to be members of this Christian Congregation, and give you, in its name, the right hand of Christian fellowship and love, and authorize you to join with us in the celebration of the Lord's Supper, and to participate in all our spiritual privileges, so long as you remain faithful to your present profession and promises. Go in peace.

Let us pray:

ALMIGHTY and most merciful God, Father of our Lord Jesus Christ, of whom the whole family in heaven and earth is named; thou hast graciously permitted us to witness a solemn renewal of the covenant with thee. Thy Church would render praise unto thee for this thy mercy, and with one voice would say: O give thanks unto the Lord; for he is good; for his mercy endureth for ever. For the mountains shall depart, and the hills be removed; but my kindness shall not depart from thee, neither shall the covenant of my peace be removed :—thus hast thou spoken, O Lord, our Redeemer.

We would now with one accord beseech thee, that thou wouldst keep these thy young servants, who have here renewed their baptismal covenant, as living members of Christ Jesus, steadfast in the true faith, and in obedience unto thy holy gospel. Strengthen them by thy Spirit, that neither false doctrine, fleshly lusts, nor the vanities of the world, may lead them astray from that truth which this day they have solemnly confessed. Grant them grace that they may grow up into him in all things, which is the head, even Christ; and evermore increase in wisdom, holiness, and righteousness, which is well-pleasing in thy sight. May they abide in thy love, and their whole life be a true confession of thy name, to their own everlasting salvation, and to the joy of their friends, to the building up of thy church, and to the praise of thy glorious grace. May they now go forth in the peace of Christ, and in the joy of the Holy Ghost, being blessed of thee, Lord, who hast made the heavens and the earth, and who hast reconciled heaven and earth.

The Congregation shall say:

Amen.

LORD Jesus Christ, true Shepherd and Bishop of our souls, who for the redemption of thy people, livest and reignest to all eternity; sanctify us all by thy grace. May we all to-day renew our vows of everlasting fidelity to thee our Lord and our Redeemer. Give us might and strength to fight a good fight, to finish our course, to keep the faith, that there may be laid up for us the crown of righteousness, which thou hast promised unto all them that love thy appearing. Let thy Spirit, and thy peace be upon us and upon our children.

We now commend ourselves to the fullness of thy grace, O Lord, our God, Father, Son, and Holy Ghost, who art able to do exceeding abundantly above all that we ask or think—unto thee be adoration, and praise, and thanksgiving, in the church, by Christ Jesus, throughout all ages, world without end.

The Congregation shall say:

Amen.

III.
The Order of Confession and Absolution,

PREPARATORY TO THE

CELEBRATION OF THE LORD'S SUPPER.

The General Confession *shall begin with an appropriate Hymn, after which shall follow prayer and the reading of the Scriptures. The Minister shall then exhort those who intend to commune to careful self-examination, and to humble and hearty confession; immediately after which exhortation he shall demand of them as here followeth:*

DEARLY Beloved. I ask you, before the omniscient God, and upon the evidence of your own conscience:

1. Whether you are truly sensible, and with contrite hearts acknowledge and lament, not only that you are by nature sinners, but that you have in various ways, by the omission of duty, and by sinful thoughts, desires, words, and actions, grieved and offended the Lord your God and Saviour, and that you have deserved that he should banish you from his presence and condemn you to everlasting punishment?

If this be your sincere conviction, confess it by saying: Yes.

Congregation.—Yes.

2. I ask you: Whether you truly believe that Jesus Christ has come into the world to save sinners, and that all who believe in his name do receive the forgiveness of their sins? Is it, therefore, your fervent desire to be delivered from your sins and guilt; and are you persuaded that our heavenly Father is willing, for Jesus Christ's sake, to be gracious unto you,

to forgive you all your sins, to cleanse you from all unrighteousness, and to sanctify you unto himself?

If this be your sincere belief, confess it by saying: Yes.

Congregation.—Yes.

3. I ask you: Whether you are fully resolved henceforth to submit yourselves to the gracious direction of the Holy Spirit, that so you may evermore strive to hate and forsake all manner of evil, to walk circumspectly before God, and daily to grow in holiness of heart and life?

If this be your serious purpose, answer, Yes.

Congregation.—Yes.

Then, all kneeling, the Minister shall say the Confession, as here followeth:

WE, poor sinners, confess unto thee, O God, our heavenly Father, that we have grievously, and in various ways, sinned against thee; not only by outward and gross sin, but by inward blindness of heart, unbelief, doubt, despondency, impatience, pride, selfishness, carnal lusts, avarice, envy, hatred and malice, and by other sinful passions, which are naked and open in thy sight, O Lord, but which we cannot fully understand, or confess unto thee. But we do sincerely repent, and are heartily sorry for these our misdoings, and we fervently implore thy forgiveness and favor, through thy dear Son Jesus Christ; being firmly resolved, by the help of the Holy Spirit, to amend our sinful lives. To this end, O God, do thou, of thy great goodness, bestow thy Holy Spirit abundantly upon us. And especially prepare us now for the worthy celebration of the Lord's Supper, so that eating of that bread, and drinking of that cup, we may be strengthened in faith and obedience toward thee, and in active charity toward our brethren of mankind.

Then shall the Congregation say:

Lord God, the Father in heaven, have mercy upon us! Lord God, the Son, Redeemer of the world, have mercy upon us! Lord God, the Holy Ghost, have mercy upon us, and grant us thy peace! Amen.

Then shall the Minister pronounce the Absolution with the Retention.

UPON this humble confession which you have now made, by virtue of my office as a Minister of our Lord Jesus Christ, I declare unto all who do truly repent and heartily believe in Jesus Christ, and are sincerely resolved to amend your sinful lives, the forgiveness of all your sins: in the name of the Father, and of the Son, and of the Holy Ghost.

But on the other hand, on the authority of the word of God, and in the name of Jesus Christ our Lord, I declare unto all who are impenitent, the hypocritical as well as the openly wicked, that so long as you continue in your impenitence, God will not forgive you your sins, but will retain them against you, and will assuredly punish you for your iniquities in the end; except you repent before your day of grace be ended, except you sincerely renounce and forsake all your evil ways and come unto Christ in true penitence and faith; which we fervently pray you may do ere it be too late.

May God have mercy upon every one of us, pardon and deliver us from all our sins, confirm and strengthen us in all goodness, and finally bring us to everlasting life, through Jesus Christ our Lord. *Amen.*

The service is then concluded by the singing of a Hymn and the Benediction.

IV.
The Order of Marriage.

DEARLY Beloved, forasmuch as marriage was instituted by God himself, and is honorable in all, it becomes those who would enter into this estate duly to weigh what the Scripture saith concerning it. Let us, therefore, for the glory of God, and for the instruction, admonition, and comfort of these persons here present, hear some portions of Scripture thereto pertaining.

In the second chapter of Genesis we read: "The Lord God said, It is not good that the man should be alone; I will make a help meet for him. Therefore shall a man leave his father and his mother, and shall cleave unto his wife; and they shall be one flesh."

Hear also the Lord's command concerning this estate. St. Paul writes, (Ephes. v. 25,) "Husbands, love your wives, even as Christ also loved the Church, and gave himself for it. So ought men to love their wives as their own bodies; he that loveth his wife loveth himself. For no man ever yet hated his own flesh; but nourisheth and cherisheth it; even as the Lord the Church. Wives, submit yourselves unto your own husbands, as unto the Lord. For the husband is the head of the wife, even as Christ is the head of the Church. Therefore, as the Church is subject unto Christ, so let the wives be to their own husbands in every thing."

But you should also remember, that by reason of our manifold sins, God has appointed that those who enter into this estate should also bear the cross. You cannot therefore expect always to enjoy prosperity; days of adversity will also come; but if you fear God and keep his commandments, he will not forsake you. He will strengthen and keep you in every time of need, and comfort you in all your sorrows.

Having now been shown what the word of God teaches concerning Marriage, I exhort you diligently to consider the same, and to strive to conform your lives thereto.

As no impediments have been shown, why you may not be lawfully joined together in matrimony; I ask you, in the presence of God, and of these witnesses :

N. DO you take this woman to your wedded wife, to live together after God's ordinance in the holy estate of matrimony. Will you love her, comfort her, honor and keep her, as a faithful christian husband is bound to do, in health and in sickness, in prosperity and in adversity; and forsaking all others, keep you only unto her, so long as you both shall live ?

Answer, *Yes*.

N. DO you take this man to your wedded husband, to live together after God's ordinance in the holy estate of matrimony; Will you love him, comfort him, honor and keep him, as a faithful christian wife is bound to do, in health and in sickness, in prosperity and in adversity; and forsaking all others, keep you only unto him, so long as you both do live ?

Answer, *Yes*.

The parties shall now join their right hands, when the Minister shall say :

WHAT God hath joined together, let no man put asunder. Forasmuch as N. and N. have consented together in holy wedlock, and have witnessed the same before God and this company, I pronounce that they are man and wife, in the name of the Father, and of the Son, and of the Holy Ghost. *Amen.*

Let us pray.

ALMIGHTY and most merciful God, who didst institute the holy estate of matrimony, and in thy good providence dost permit these thy servants to enter into the same; we render thee most hearty thanks for this thy goodness: and we beseech thee to grant them thy grace, that they may lead a truly christian and godly life, in accordance with the teachings of thy holy word. Let thy heavenly blessing abide upon them, that they may be defended from all temptations to sin, and be kept from all danger and harm. Remove from them all discord and contention; strengthen them to constant fidelity and sincere affection towards each other; and preserve them, with all thy true followers, in steadfastness of faith, in the knowledge of thy dear Son, and in patience under trials to the end of their lives; for the sake of our Saviour Jesus Christ, who liveth and reigneth with thee, in the unity of the Holy Spirit, ever one God. *Amen.*

OUR Father, who art in heaven; Hallowed be thy name; Thy kingdom come; Thy will be done on earth, as it is in heaven; Give us this day our daily bread; And forgive us our trespasses, as we forgive those who trespass against us; And lead us not into temptation; But deliver us from evil; For thine is the kingdom, and the power, and the glory, for ever and ever. *Amen.*

V.
The Order for the Communion of the Sick.

The Minister should address the sick person, explaining the nature and design of the Lord's Supper, and the state of soul requisite to a worthy reception of the same. He may then use the Order of Confession and Absolution, and of the Holy Communion as before given, with such alterations as the circumstances require, or he may use the following Order:

THE Lord be with you!

BELOVED Brother (*Sister*,) in Christ! You desire to receive the Holy Supper of our Lord Jesus Christ, for the comfort and strengthening of your soul. You should come to this Sacrament with a due sense of the vanity of all earthly things, of which your sickness forcibly reminds you; with serious reflections on the hour, (perhaps near at hand,) of your departure from this world; and with solemn thoughts of that eternity toward which we are hastening. In order that you may worthily partake of this Sacrament to your profit, be mindful of the exhortation of the Apostle: "Let a man examine himself, and so let him eat of that bread, and drink of that cup." Remember also the words, "If we say that we have no sin, we deceive ourselves, and the truth is not in us. But if we confess our sins, God is faithful and just to forgive us our sins, and to cleanse us from all unrighteousness." Draw nigh therefore to God with an humble and penitent heart, and beseech him to grant you his grace for Jesus Christ's sake, and confess your sins unto him, saying:

ALMIGHTY God, my heavenly Father, I come before thee deeply humbled on account of my manifold sins. I will confess them unto thee with sincere sorrow and heartfelt penitence; and I desire to find peace for my soul, through faith in thy dear Son, whom thou hast delivered up to suffer and die that he might redeem the world. O sanctify unto me this memorial of his atoning death which I desire now to keep. O God of all mercy, grant, and seal unto me the blessed assurance that thou wilt not remember my sins against me; but for the sake of my dear Saviour, vouchsafe unto me the forgiveness of all my sins, and let thy fatherly mercy be upon me. It is my serious purpose to serve thee with filial gratitude and faithfulness, and to do and suffer thy holy will to the end of my days. Do thou graciously strengthen me, by thy mighty power, in carrying this purpose into effect. O God, my hope is in thee; have mercy upon me, and give me thy peace. *Amen.*

In order that you may yourself confirm this confession; I ask you:

Do you humbly acknowledge and heartily lament your sins? Do you believe that God, your merciful Father, will, for the sake of Jesus Christ your Saviour, pardon all your offences? And are you resolved, should God prolong your days, to lead the residue of your life in his fear and to his glory? Then declare it before the Omniscient God by saying: *Yes.*

According to your faith be it unto you. By command of our Lord Jesus Christ, I announce unto you the divine promise of the forgiveness of all your sins; in the name of the Father, and of the Son, and of the Holy Ghost. *Amen.*

Let us now, in the name of Jesus Christ, and in accordance with his institution, consecrate this bread and wine, and truly keep his holy Supper.

Then shall the Minister proceed as in the Order of the Holy Communion, saying the Lord's Prayer and the words of Institution, after which he shall say:

O LAMB of God, who though most innocent, wast slain upon the cross; who didst patiently and meekly bear the contradiction of sinners, and the cruelty of thy enemies; except thou hadst borne our sins, we must for ever despair; have mercy upon us, O Christ.

DEAR Brother! (Sister,) come now to this gracious Supper, and be made one with your Lord and Saviour; and may you receive from him, by virtue of such blessed union, peace of conscience, patience under affliction, steadfastness in the hour of death, and the foretaste of everlasting happiness. Look upon him, who though unseen is present with us, and in whom all the promises of God are yea and amen. Behold, he standeth at the door of your heart and knocketh, if you will hear his voice and open the door, he will come in to you, and will sup with you and you with him.

The Distribution shall then follow as in the Order of the Holy Communion before given. The Minister shall then say:

BLESS the Lord, O my soul; and all that is within me, bless his holy name. Bless the Lord, O my soul, and forget not all his benefits; who forgiveth all thine iniquities; who healeth all thy diseases; who redeemeth thy life from destruction; and who crowneth thee with loving-kindness and tender mercies. O God, my heavenly Father, I thank thee that thou hast refreshed me with the holy Supper of my Saviour. What am I, that thou dost esteem me worthy to receive so precious a seal of thy grace. The life which I now live in the flesh, I will live by the faith of the Son of God, who loved me, and gave himself for me. With confident faith I commend my soul to thee, most merciful God, my Creator. Thou wilt not forsake me while I live in this world; thou wilt in mercy remember all my household; and when my last hour shall come, thou wilt redeem me from all evil, and bring me to thy heavenly kingdom. Cause now this heavenly food so to strengthen and keep me, in faith and love, in patience and hope, that I may with childlike trust submit to thy fatherly will, give praises to thy holy name even under trials and sufferings, and living or dying, continue thine for ever in body and soul, through Jesus Christ, my Saviour. *Amen.*

The Lord bless thee, and keep thee;

The Lord make his face shine upon thee, and be gracious unto thee.

The Lord lift up his countenance upon thee, and give thee peace. *Amen.*

VI.
The Order for the Burial of the Dead.

The order of the parts of the Burial Service may be varied as circumstances require. At the house of the deceased, if the Service is begun there, or at the place of Burial, the Minister shall say:

I AM the resurrection and the life, saith the Lord: he that believeth in me, though he were dead, yet shall he live: and whosoever liveth and believeth in me, shall never die.

We brought nothing into this world, and it is certain we can carry nothing out. The Lord gave, and the Lord hath taken away; blessed be the name of the Lord.

Blessed are the dead which die in the Lord from henceforth: Yea, saith the Spirit, that they may rest from their labors; and their works do follow them.

If the Service is begun at the house of the deceased, a verse may now be sung, after which the Minister may say:

LET us now attend the mortal remains of our deceased brother, [sister, child,] in christian order, to their last resting place.

If an address is made at the grave, it may now follow. The Minister, standing at the grave, shall then say:

MAN, that is born of woman, is of few days, and full of trouble. He cometh forth like a flower, and is cut down: he fleeth also as a shadow, and continueth not.

In the midst of life we are in death: of whom may we seek for succor, but of thee, O Lord, who for our sins art justly displeased?

Yet, O Lord God most holy, O Lord most mighty,

O holy and most merciful Saviour, deliver us not into the bitter pains of eternal death.

Thou knowest, Lord, the secrets of our hearts; shut not thy merciful ears to our prayers; but spare us, Lord most holy, O God most mighty, O holy and merciful Saviour, thou most worthy Judge eternal, suffer us not, at our last hour, for any pains of death, to fall from thee.

After the corpse is laid in the grave the Minister shall say:

FORASMUCH as it hath pleased Almighty God, in his wise providence, to take out of this world the soul of our deceased brother, (sister,) we therefore commit his (her) body to the ground; earth to earth, ashes to ashes, dust to dust; in the sure and certain hope of the resurrection to eternal life, through our Lord Jesus Christ, who shall change our vile body, that it may be like unto his glorious body, and receive us into his eternal kingdom.

If the Burial Service is to be continued and ended in the Church, a portion of a Hymn shall be sung, when the Minister shall say one or more of the Collects here following, after which all shall go to the Church. The following Scripture Lessons are suitable to be read in the church; 1 Thess. iv. 13–18. 1 Cor. xv. 20–57. 2 Cor. v. 1–10. Rev. vii. 9–17. Job xix. 25–27. Psalms xxxi., xxxiv., xxxix., xlii. lxxi., lxxiii., xc., cxxxix. John v. 24–29. vi. 37–40. xi. 1–44. Luke vii. 11–25. Mat. ix. 18–25.

1.

O GOD, our heavenly Father, who hast taught us by thy holy Apostle, not to be sorry, as men without hope, for those who sleep in Jesus; mercifully grant unto us, that after this life, we may be received, with all those who are departed in the true faith, into thy everlasting glory; through Jesus Christ our Lord. Amen.

2.

ALMIGHTY God, who by the death of thy Son hast abolished sin and death, and by his resurrection has brought life and immortality to light, to the end that we should be delivered from the dominion of the devil, and that by the power of the same resurrection, our mortal bodies should be raised up from the dead, and live with thee in thy kingdom; mercifully grant, that with our whole heart we may believe this comfortable truth, and finally, with all thy saints, come to the blessed resurrection of the just; through the same our Lord Jesus Christ, who liveth and reigneth with thee and the Holy Ghost, for ever and ever. Amen.

3.

O LORD Jesus Christ, who wilt come again in glorious majesty, to judge the quick and the dead, and whose voice all who sleep in the graves shall hear, and come forth, either to the reward of life eternal, or to the sentence of condemnation; we humbly beseech thee that thou wouldst be gracious unto us, and raise us up unto eternal life, so that we may receive that blessing which thou shalt then pronounce to all who love and fear thee, saying: Come, ye blessed of my Father, inherit the kingdom prepared for you from the foundation of the world. And to thee be praise, for ever and ever. Amen.

4.

ETERNAL and unchangeable God, by whose providence we have been called to witness this instance of mortality, and in whose hand is the life of every human being: enable us, we beseech thee, to lay to heart the serious lessons, which are now addressed to us. Teach us so to number our days, that we may apply our hearts unto wisdom, set our affections upon the things which are above, perform without delay the great work which thou hast given us to do, live by the faith of thy Son, and habitually look forward to his second coming. Comfort and support the spirits of thy servants, who mourn over this afflicting dispensation. Let their hearts be stayed upon thee, and rejoice in the precious discoveries of thy word. And let them find by their own experience, that all things work together for good to them that love thee. Amen.

THE BENEDICTION.

VII.
The Order for the Installation of the Church Council.

DEAR Brethren: You have been duly elected by the members of this Church as its officers. As your brethren have thus shown that they confide in your readiness to discharge with fidelity the offices to which you have been chosen, in a manner satisfactory to themselves, and consistent with your christian obligations, and so as you will desire to have done when God shall call you to your last account, I now ask your attention to a brief statement of your official duties.

I. *The duties of Elders are these:*

1. They shall set before the Church a truly christian example.

2. They shall take care that evangelical doctrine and christian discipline are maintained and perpetuated in the Church.

3. They shall visit the schools of the Church from time to time, and see that good order is observed in them, and that the children are properly instructed.

4. When discord and controversies arise, they shall endeavor, as far as possible, to reconcile the parties concerned, and to restore peace.

5. If the Pastor desire it, they shall accompany him in his visits to the sick.

6. They shall see that all the temporal affairs of the Church are duly attended to and administered, and aid in the execution of any measures adapted to promote its well-being.

II. *The duties of Deacons are these:*

1. They shall set the Church an example of a truly christian life.

2. They shall render all necessary aid in the services of the sanctuary, and especially in the administration of the Lord's Supper.

3. They shall take up all collections in the Church, and pay the sums collected to the Treasurer, as often as he may consider it necessary for the good of the Church.

4. It shall be their duty to see, that according to Christ's command, the minister of the Church be properly supported. And lastly, that all things connected with the public worship of God, be done decently and in order.

III. *The duties of Trustees, if the Congregation have such officers, are these:*

1. They shall endeavor, by the help of God, to set their own household and the Congregation, a worthy example by their Christian walk and conversation.

2. They shall take care that the property of the congregation is not injured or destroyed, and that the Church building is kept in good repair.

3. They shall see that the deeds, and other important papers of the Church, are carefully preserved.

4. That the debts of the Church, if it have any, are diminished and removed, in the manner most consistent with the interests of the Church.

YOU have thus heard, my brethren, what are the duties that pertain to your respective offices. In order that the congregation may be certified of your willingness to perform them to the best of your ability, you will now in the presence of God make known this your willingness by saying: *I will.*

Let us pray.

THE INSTALLATION OF THE CHURCH COUNCIL. 187

LORD Jesus Christ, who art the chief Shepherd and Bishop of that flock which thou hast purchased with thy blood, we thank thee that thou hast established thy Church upon the earth, and that amidst many persecutions and violent assaults, thou hast hitherto protected it against the gates of hell, and more and more extended it among men. We thank thee that we also have been born within this Church, and been invited through thy gospel to the blessedness of communion with thee; that we are in the enjoyment of the means of grace, and of the operations of thy Holy Spirit. We thank thee that thou continuest to dispose men to labor in thy Church, and faithfully to provide for its temporal and its spiritual welfare. Blessed Saviour, it is the Church which thou hast purchased with thy blood. Continue to bless and preserve it we beseech thee; and let thy word dwell in thy people richly in all wisdom, and make it powerful to carry on thy work of grace in our souls. Vouchsafe thy grace and favor unto these brethren who have been duly elected to important offices in this Church, and who are now before thee, in order to take upon them the solemn responsibilities of their several stations. Enlighten and guide them by thy Holy Spirit, that they may know thy mind, and that their services to the Church may redound to its good and to thy praise. Fill their hearts with love to thee, to thy word, and to their brethren whom they are to instruct by their example, and to aid by their counsels and their active services; that so, ever seeking help from thee by faith, they may with alacrity and cheerfulness, perform the duties of the several offices to which they have been set apart. Hear, O Lord, and answer our prayers, for the sake of that love wherewith thou lovest us. *Amen.*

The Minister, giving his right hand to each, shall say:

I WISH you the blessing and guidance of God in the exercise of your office. May the Lord direct and assist you by his Holy Spirit; may he counsel and strengthen you in all your undertakings, and encourage you to labor diligently for the prosperity of this Church, and to fulfill with fidelity your respective duties. And be assured that he who is faithful and just to reward those who serve him with uprightness and fidelity, will bless your labors, and grant you in time and eternity, a recompense, according to his great goodness. Depart in peace.

The Minister, turning now to those who are going out of office, shall say:

I ADDRESS myself to you, dear brethren, who are now retiring from office, and tender you the thanks of the congregation, for the faithfulness and zeal which you have manifested in its service. That the Lord may bless and reward you, is the sincere wish and prayer of us all.

VIII.

The Order for the Opening and the Closing of the Synod.

COLLECT *to be used after the Collect for the day at the Morning Service which precedes the Opening of Synod.*

ALMIGHTY God, our heavenly Father, we humbly beseech thee, with thy favor to behold thy servants, here assembled, to prepare for holy and important labors in behalf of thy Church. Without thee we can do nothing; grant us therefore thy grace and strength, and let thy blessing so rest upon our endeavors, that they may tend to thy honor, and to the furtherance of thy kingdom on earth.

Lord Jesus Christ, thou Lord and Head of the Church, who hast promised to be with us alway, even unto the end of the world; make thy glorious presence now manifest among us, and do thou so govern and strengthen all the ministers and members of thy Church, by the power of thy grace, that both in word and deed, they may cheerfully and steadfastly confess thy name before the world.

O Holy Spirit, thou Spirit of the Father and the Son, descend upon us with thy heavenly gifts; send out thy light and thy truth, let them lead us in all our ways, that we may not dread the account, which we shall have to render to the Judge of the living and the dead.

Most holy Trinity, Father, Son, and Holy Ghost, be favorable unto us, and prosper thy work in our hands. Save now, we beseech thee, O Lord: O Lord, we beseech thee, send now prosperity. *Amen.*

The Opening of the Synod.

A Hymn of Invocation of the Holy Spirit, or any suitable Hymn shall be sung, after which shall be said as follows:

The President:
The Lord be with you.

The Members of the Synod shall answer:
And with thy Spirit.

The President:
Holy, holy, holy, is the Lord our God.

The Members of the Synod shall answer:
Heaven and earth are full of his glory.

The President:
Let us pray:

HOLY art thou, O Lord, heavenly Father, who dwellest in the high and holy place; we are unholy and wait for thy salvation. Grant us now that grace which thou hast promised, which thy Son has purchased, which thy Holy Spirit conveys, and which all those who earnestly beseech thee therefor, shall assuredly receive. We humble ourselves before the throne of thy grace in lowliness of heart, and implore of thee, the gifts of thy Holy Spirit, the Spirit of truth and of wisdom, of power and of might, of love and of concord. May he remove all self-sufficiency and all arrogance from us, the ministers of thy Church and heralds of thy gospel, and keep us from being led astray through selfishness and sinful desires. May he sanctify us through thy truth. May he so reign and rule within us, that we, being filled with strength and courage, may continually seek after this one thing: to do thy holy will, to glorify thy Son, and to build up thy kingdom. May he himself make intercession for us, with groanings which cannot be uttered, and direct us in all our deliberations and decisions to Jesus Christ, who ever liveth and reigneth with thee and the Holy Spirit, one God, world without end.

The Members of Synod shall say:

Amen.

Then shall the First Assistant, followed by the Members of Synod, say:

I BELIEVE in God the Father Almighty, Maker of heaven and earth.

And in Jesus Christ his only Son, our Lord; Who was conceived by the Holy Ghost, Born of the Virgin Mary; Suffered under Pontius Pilate, Was crucified, dead, and buried; He descended into hell; The third day he rose again from the dead; He ascended into heaven, And sitteth on the right hand of God the Father Almighty; From thence he shall come to judge the quick and the dead.

I believe in the Holy Ghost; The holy Christian Church, the Communion of Saints; The forgiveness of sins; The Resurrection of the body; And the life everlasting. Amen.

Then shall the Second Assistant, followed by the Members of Synod, say:

OUR Father, who art in heaven; Hallowed be thy name; Thy kingdom come; Thy will be done on earth, as it is in heaven; Give us this day our daily bread; And forgive us our trespasses, as we forgive those who trespass against us; And lead us not into temptation; But deliver us from evil; For thine is the kingdom, and the power, and the glory, for ever and ever. Amen.

The President:

HAVING therefore, dear brethren, boldness to enter into the holiest by the blood of Jesus, and having an high priest over the house of God; let us draw near with a true heart, in full assurance of faith, having our hearts sprinkled from an evil conscience. And let us hold fast the profession of our faith without wavering; for he is faithful that promised. And let us consider one another, to provoke unto love, and to good works.

I DO hereby open this Synod, in accordance with the usage and principles of our Evangelical Lutheran Church; for the glory of God, for the welfare of the Church of Jesus Christ, and for the edification of all who believe in his name; In the name of the Father, and of the Son, and of the Holy Ghost. *Amen.*

The Lord be with us, that we may prove what is that good, and acceptable, and perfect will of God.

The Members of the Synod shall say:
Amen.

The Closing of the Synod.

A Hymn of praise and thanksgiving shall be sung, after which shall be said as follows:

The President:
O give thanks unto the Lord, for he is good:

The Members of Synod:
And his mercy endureth for ever.

The President:
Let us pray:

ALMIGHTY and most merciful God, who art the source of all light and of all truth, we give thanks unto thee, and laud thy holy name, that thou hast graciously granted us the assistance and comfort of thy good Spirit, to the end that we might be preserved from the blinding influence of error, worldly-mindedness, and vanity. And we pray that thy Spirit may continue so to rule and govern us, that strong in the power of faith, and unmovable in steadfastness of heart, we may persevere in thy work, and may always be found as faithful laborers in thy vineyard, and as fearless confessors of thy truth, unto the day of the coming of thy Son, our Lord and Saviour Jesus Christ.

The Members of Synod shall say:

Amen.

The President:

I DO now close this Synod, in the name of the Lord. And now, dear brethren, let us stand fast in the love of Christ, that when he comes again in his glory, we may not be put to shame, but rejoice before him.

The First Assistant, followed by the Members of Synod, shall say:

I BELIEVE in God the Father Almighty, Maker of heaven and earth.

And in Jesus Christ his only Son, our Lord; Who was conceived by the Holy Ghost, Born of the Virgin Mary; Suffered under Pontius Pilate, Was crucified, dead, and buried; He descended into hell; The third day he rose again from the dead; He ascended into heaven, And sitteth on the right hand of God the Father Almighty; From thence he shall come to judge the quick and the dead.

I believe in the Holy Ghost; The holy Christian Church, the Communion of Saints; The forgiveness of sins; The Resurrection of the body; And the life everlasting. Amen.

The Second Assistant, followed by the Members of Synod, shall say:

OUR Father, who art in heaven; Hallowed be thy name; Thy kingdom come; Thy will be done on earth, as it is in heaven; Give us this day our daily bread; And forgive us our trespasses, as we forgive those who trespass against us; And lead us not into temptation; But deliver us from evil; For thine is the kingdom, and the power, and the glory, for ever and ever. *Amen.*

The President:

The grace of our Lord Jesus Christ, the love of God, and the communion of the Holy Ghost be with you all.

The Members of Synod shall say:

Amen.

Luther's Hymn, "A safe stronghold our God is still," or another Hymn of like import may then be sung.

IX.
The Order of Ordination to the Office of the Ministry.

ORDINATION *usually takes place before the assembled Synod, but should any Congregation desire that its Minister be ordained in the Church where he is called to serve, and be willing to bear the costs, the request should be granted. If the Officers of Synod cannot attend the Ordination, the President shall appoint a Committee for this purpose. A sermon on the office of the ministry should be preached; if this cannot be done, an address at the Altar should precede the Ordination.*

After the sermon, a Hymn of invocation of the Holy Spirit should be sung. At the close of the Hymn, the Ordaining Minister and the Assistants shall go to the Altar, and the persons to be ordained shall stand before it. The Ordaining Minister shall say:

IN the name of the Father, and of the Son, and of the Holy Ghost.

Or this:

The grace of our Lord Jesus Christ, the love of God, and the communion of the Holy Ghost be with you all.

DEARLY Beloved, forasmuch as the Lord, of his great goodness, has called these Christian brethren here present, to be Ministers of his Church, we have assembled, that in accordance with apostolic usage, we may ordain and consecrate them, by the laying on of hands, and prayer. Before we proceed to this solemn act of consecration, we will set before you, dear brethren in the Lord, what the Scriptures teach concerning the office of those, who are called to be faithful preachers of the word, and to have the care of souls, that ye may know how to approve yourselves as servants that need not be ashamed before the Lord, the chief Shepherd of his sheep.

Our Lord Jesus Christ, after his resurrection, said to his disciples, (John xx. 21,) Peace be unto you: as my Father hath sent me, even so send I you.

When he was about to ascend into heaven, he said unto them, (Mat. xxviii. 18,) All power is given unto me in heaven and in earth. Go ye therefore, and teach all nations, baptizing them in the name of the Father, and of the Son, and of the Holy Ghost; teaching them to observe all things whatsoever I have commanded you: and lo, I am with you alway, even unto the end of the world.

And when he ascended up far above all heavens, that he might fill all things; he gave some, apostles; and some, prophets; and some, evangelists; and some, pastors and teachers; for the perfecting of the saints, for the work of the ministry, for the edifying of the body of Christ. (Eph. iv. 10.)

Therefore the office of the ministry of reconciliation, the office of the Spirit whose work it is to justify, to renew, and to save, was instituted by the Lord himself. Not that they are sufficient of themselves to hold this Office of the New Testament, but their sufficiency is of God. They are ambassadors for Christ; as though God did beseech you by them; and they have received from God a ministration of exceeding glory.

They should therefore adorn their ministry in all things, as St. Paul the apostle writes to Timothy and Titus. A bishop must be blameless, the husband of one wife; one that ruleth well his own house, having his children in subjection with all gravity; (for if a man know not how to rule his own house, how shall he take care of the Church of God?) not self-willed, not soon angry, vigilant, sober, not given to wine, no striker, not greedy of filthy lucre, of good behavior, temperate, just, holy, given to hospitality, a lover of good men, not a brawler, not covetous, but patient, not a novice, lest being lifted up with pride he fall into the condemnation of the devil, apt to teach, holding fast the faithful word as he hath been taught, that he may be able by sound doctrine both to exhort and to convince the gainsayers. Moreover, he must have a good report of them which are without; lest he fall into reproach and the snare of the devil. He must be an example of the believers, in word, in conversation, in charity, in spirit, in faith, in purity. He must give attendance to reading, to exhortation, to doctrine; and not neglect the gift that is in him, which was given him by prophecy, with the laying on of the hands of the presbytery. He must meditate upon these things, and give himself wholly to them; that his profiting may appear to all. He must take heed unto himself, and unto the doctrine, and continue in them: for in so doing he shall both save himself and them that hear him. The same blessed apostle has briefly set forth all these things in his charge to the elders at Ephesus, Acts xx. 28, where he says: Take heed therefore unto yourselves, and to all the flock, over the which the Holy Ghost hath made you overseers, to feed the Church of God, which he hath purchased with his own blood.

From all these things ye learn to how high a dignity, and to how weighty an Office and charge, ye are called; and that it is most certainly true, what the apostle saith: If a man desire the office of a bishop, he desireth a good work. Forasmuch then as your Office and work is of so great difficulty, and ye are not able of yourselves faithfully to fulfill it, so as shall be well pleasing to God, and to the edification of the Church; we exhort you to put your trust in the almighty grace of Jesus Christ our Lord, and to comfort yourselves with his help. They that wait upon the Lord shall renew their strength. And he who has promised to be with us alway, even unto the end of the world, will uphold you, and prosper you, in that whereunto he has sent you. And may he, whose strength is made perfect in our weakness, now give you grace, with pure lips, and sincere hearts, to make that confession which the Church has authorized us to ask of you. To this end lift up your hearts unto God, and say:

FATHER of our Lord Jesus Christ, I beseech thee to strengthen me now by thy good Spirit, that with gladness and sincerity of heart, I may confess my purpose to serve thee in doctrine and life; so that ever hereafter this hour may be blessed unto my soul. Out of the depths do I cry unto thee, O Lord. Lord, hear my voice: let thine ears be attentive to the voice of my supplications. I wait for the Lord, my soul doth wait, and in his word do I hope. Amen.

I NOW demand of you, beloved brethren in the Lord, in the presence of God and our Lord Jesus Christ, and also of this christian assembly: Whether you are now ready, after due consideration, to take upon you this holy Office, and as God shall give you strength, to execute and discharge the same, in such manner as shall be well pleasing to the Lord and Chief Shepherd of the Church? Will you preach the pure word of God, in accordance with the true understanding of the same, as set forth in the Confessions of our Church; and will you, by the grace of God, set to others the example of a godly life? If you so purpose, confess it before God, and this christian congregation, by your solemn assent.

The persons to be ordained shall then say:
(one after the other)

YES, with my whole heart, the Lord helping me, through the power and grace of his Holy Spirit.

Then shall the Ordaining Minister say:

YOU have witnessed a good confession before many witnesses, whereunto we say, Yea and Amen. Kneel down before the omnipresent God, and receive with prayer and supplication this holy consecration.

The persons to be ordained humbly kneeling, the Ordaining Minister shall say:

UPON these solemn vows, which you have now taken upon you before God and men; we beseech God, the Father of our blessed Lord and Saviour Jesus Christ, the only Lord of the harvest, that he would so replenish you with his Holy Spirit, that you may be fitted worthily to exercise this sacred Office. May he so strengthen and keep you, that you may give no offence in any thing, that the ministry be not blamed; but in all things approve yourselves as the ministers of God, in much patience, in afflictions, in necessities, in distresses, in labors, in watchings, in fastings; by pureness, by knowledge, by long-suffering, by kindness, by the Holy Ghost, by love unfeigned, by the armor of righteousness on the right hand and on the left, by honor and dishonor, by evil report and good report; as deceivers, and yet true; as unknown, and yet well known; as dying, and behold, ye live; as chastened, and not killed; as sorrowful, yet always rejoicing; as poor, yet making many rich; as having nothing, yet possessing all things. (2 Cor. vi.)—The Lord grant you grace to do and suffer the work of the gospel ministry, that in that great day ye may be ready to appear before the judgment seat of our Lord Jesus Christ, to give answer to the righteous Judge, to receive from his hand glory and honor and immortality, and to shine as the brightness of the firmament, and as the stars forever and ever. Amen.

The Assisting Ministers shall say:

Amen. Amen.

ORDINATION.

Then the Ordaining Minister, with the Assistants, shall lay their hands severally upon the head of every one to be ordained, the Ordaining Minister saying:

WE now commit unto thee, by the imposition of our hands, the holy Office of the Word and the Sacraments of the Triune God; we ordain and consecrate thee to a Minister in the Church, in the name of the Father, and of the Son, and of the Holy Ghost.

The Assisting Ministers shall say:

Amen. Amen.

Then shall all the Ministers together say:

OUR Father who art in heaven; Hallowed be thy name; Thy kingdom come; Thy will be done on earth, as it is in heaven; Give us this day our daily bread; And forgive us our trespasses, as we forgive those who trespass against us; And lead us not into temptation; But deliver us from evil; For thine is the kingdom, and the power, and the glory, for ever and ever. Amen.

The Ordaining Minister alone shall then say:

MOST merciful God, our heavenly Father, through the mouth of thy dear Son our Lord Jesus Christ, thou hast declared: " The harvest truly is great, but the laborers are few; pray ye therefore the Lord of the harvest, that he would send forth laborers into his harvest." In obedience to this thy command, we humbly and heartily beseech thee, plenteously to endow these thy servants, us, and all who are called to the Office and work of thy Ministry, with thy Holy Spirit, that we, together with a great multitude, may be thy faithful Evangelists, and continue steadfast against all the temptations of the world, the flesh, and the devil, to the end, that through our endeavors thy name may be hallowed, thy kingdom be extended, and thy will be done on earth. May it please thee to restrain and bring to nought all thy enemies, who blaspheme thy name, and hinder thy kingdom; and wherever thy servants preach and labor, do thou bless their preaching, and prosper the work of their hands and hearts, to the praise of thy most holy name, and to the salvation of souls; through thy dear Son our Lord Jesus Christ, who liveth and reigneth with thee and the Holy Ghost, world without end.

The Congregation shall say:

Amen.

The Ordaining Minister shall then say to the persons ordained:

GO then, and feed the flock of God which is among you, taking the oversight thereof, not by constraint but willingly; not for filthy lucre, but of a ready mind; not as being lords over God's heritage, but being ensamples to the flock. And when the chief Shepherd shall appear, ye shall receive a crown of glory that fadeth not away. The Lord bless you from on high, and make you a blessing unto many, that you may bring forth fruit, and that your fruit may remain unto eternal life.

The persons ordained shall say:

Amen.

Then shall be sung a Hymn of praise and thanksgiving.—*If the Lord's Supper is administered, it shall now begin at the words of Institution.*—*If there is no communion, the services shall close with the* BENEDICTION.—*If the Ordination takes place in the Congregation of the person ordained he shall not preach at that time.*

X.

The Order for the Installation of a Minister.

If the Minister who is to be installed preaches on the occasion, the Installation should precede the sermon. But if the President of the Ministerium, or another Minister appointed by him, preaches, the Installation should follow the sermon. The officiating Minister shall begin the regular Sunday Morning Service, proceeding as far as the Collect for the day, after which, or instead of it, he shall say the Collect here following:

Let us pray.

MOST merciful God, our heavenly Father, who hast commanded us by the mouth of thy dear Son, that we should pray thee to send forth laborers into thy harvest; we earnestly beseech thee to send unto us continually true teachers and ministers of thy word, and so to enlighten their minds with the knowledge of thy truth, that they may faithfully make known the whole counsel of thy will; that we being admonished, enlightened, nourished, comforted, and strengthened by thy heavenly and everlasting word, may in this present world do those things which please thee, and finally come to the enjoyment of eternal life; through Jesus Christ, thy Son, our Lord. Amen.

Then shall the following Scripture Lessons be read instead of, or after, the Epistle and Gospel for the day: 1 Tim. iii. 1–7. vi. 3–21. Acts xx. 28–31. John xx. 21–23. If the Minister installed preaches, now, if not, at the close of the sermon, the officiating Minister standing at the Altar shall say:

IN the name of the Father, and of the Son, and of the Holy Ghost. Amen.

BELOVED brethren, members of this christian Church:—We have been duly authorized to install as your Pastor and Teacher, N. N. our esteemed brother and fellow laborer in the service of our Lord

Jesus Christ. Although we do not doubt that the Congregation have fully concurred in his election, it becomes us nevertheless to pay due regard to church order. Therefore, before we proceed to this Installation, we desire to be duly certified by the Congregation, through its council, that you have chosen this brother to be your Pastor.

This may now be done according to previous arrangement, either by the delivery to the officiating Minister of a written call, or by the oral declaration of one or more of the Church-council appointed for this purpose. Then shall the officiating Minister say:

WE now proceed with pleasure to discharge the duty entrusted to us, and request our brother to present himself before the Altar.

The Minister to be installed now presents himself before the Altar; he should be accompanied by the members of the Church-council.

RECEIVE then, dear brother, the holy Office to which you have been duly chosen by this christian Congregation. Receive it with its privileges and its responsibilities. We all entertain the confident hope that you will discharge its duties with conscientious fidelity, in the sight of God and of men. You will preach the word of the Lord in its purity, from a heart animated by faith, and administer his ordinances with pure hands. You will persevere in your inquiries after truth, and aim to render every acquisition of knowledge conducive to the end of your office. While you seek to become all things to all men, you will make it the great aim of your labors to promote true and vital godliness, and to win souls to Christ. You will regard with special interest the lambs of your flock, taking care that they are early instructed in the doctrines of the gospel, that so they may be the planting of the Lord, and flourish in the courts of our God, and thus not only attain their own salvation, but become a blessing to the Church. You will consider it the chief duty of your high calling, ever to accompany soundness of doctrine with holiness of life, setting to others a wholesome example of every christian virtue, thus showing by your whole walk and conversation, that you are truly a disciple of the Lord Jesus Christ.

You have already in your secret prayer vowed unto God to perform all these duties; and you will now announce this your purpose to the Congregation about to be committed to your charge.

I THEREFORE ask you, before the omnipresent God, the searcher of all hearts, at the sacred Altar of our Lord Jesus Christ, and in the presence of this christian Congregation; are you firmly and earnestly resolved to fulfill all the duties of your holy Office with conscientious fidelity; Will you order all your instructions according to the word of God in holy Scripture, and the Confessions of our Evangelical Lutheran Church founded on the same, and by your life and conversation show yourself a true minister of our Lord Jesus Christ? If this be your serious purpose, announce it to the Congregation by saying:

Answer. Yes, by the help of God!

Then shall the officiating Minister say:

THE Lord who hath heard your promise, grant unto you strength and power to perform the same. May he at all times enlighten you by his Spirit, comfort you with his peace, and crown your labors in his name with abundant success.

The officiating Minister, then turning to the Congregation, shall say:

DEAR brethren, members of this Congregation, receive your Pastor with that respect and love to which he is justly entitled. You have yourselves chosen him as your Pastor; and without your respect and love, he cannot prosecute the work of the Lord with success. Be mindful of the admonition of the

Apostle: "Obey them that have the rule over you, and submit yourselves: for they watch for your souls, as they that must give account: that they may do it with joy and not with grief: for that is unprofitable for you." Receive him then with fixed purpose to do everything in your power to cause him, even in eternity, to bless the day that brought him among you. Duly regard his labors in your behalf, and esteem him very highly in love for his work's sake, and be peaceably minded toward him, aiding and comforting him in his conflicts by your prayers. Happy the Congregation that rightly estimates the services of a faithful godly minister; and happy the minister upon whom the Lord hath bestowed the privilege of laboring in such a Congregation. Let us now entreat the Lord, that the connection which has this day been formed, may be thus happy and blessed, to Pastor and Congregation.

Prayer.

ALMIGHTY and everlasting Father; thou hast established a kingdom for thyself upon the earth. Thou hast founded for thyself, in thy Son Jesus, a holy Church, against which the gates of hell cannot prevail. It is thy gracious will that from this blessed institution, salvation to the souls of men shall go forth unto the end of days. Praise and adoration be unto thee, the Father of mercies, for this manifestation of thy goodness and grace.

In this place also hath the holy Altar of thy Son been erected; this house hath been raised and set apart for the assembling together of a Congregation that profess his name, and unto which the word of his redemption is preached, and the fatness of thy house is dispensed. For this we render praise and thanksgiving unto thee. Glory be to thee for all the blessings which the preaching of thy gospel in these thy courts, hath in days past brought unto immortal souls. And peace be with all who have labored in thy service within this Congregation and been faithful in their labors.

Our Father in Christ. Thou dost this day send another laborer into this thy harvest field. Thou dost command him to spread thy heavenly light, to invite men to thy heavenly consolations; in Christ's stead to beseech those whom he has redeemed: "Be ye reconciled unto God." Look down in mercy upon him, that he may fulfill his holy office here to the praise of thy glorious name. Replenish him with all those thy gifts which are requisite to the faithful and successful execution of his office. Support him in all his endeavors by thy mighty power, and crown his sincere efforts with blessed success. Give him strength to be faithful to his high calling, even amid difficulties and opposition. And when at last his work on earth is ended, may he as a faithful servant enter into the joy of his Lord.

O Lord, bless this Congregation. Bless the officers and all the members of the Church. Preserve thine Altar perpetually in their midst, and ever keep alive upon it thy holy fire. May thy word and sacraments be continued unto them in their purity, and the peaceful kingdom of thy Son so flourish and prosper, that all who worship thee in this place may in the end find their names written in the Lamb's book of life.

O Lord our God, who doest more than we can ask or think, fill us all with thy grace. O thou God of peace, sanctify us wholly, that our whole spirit and soul and body may be preserved blameless unto the coming of our Lord Jesus Christ. *Amen.*

A Hymn shall now be sung, after which the newly installed Pastor, standing with his face to the Altar, shall say:

Create in me a clean heart, O God; and renew a right spirit within me.

Turning to the congregation, he shall say:
The Lord be with you.

The Congregation shall answer:
And with thy spirit.

The Minister:
Let us pray.

MOST merciful God, our heavenly Father; give, we beseech thee, unto me, and unto this Congregation, thy holy Spirit, and christian faithfulness and wisdom. Make me a diligent and worthy teacher and servant of thy divine word, and thus build up and bless thy Church; to the end that we, being admonished, enlightened, nourished, comforted and strengthened by thy heavenly and everlasting word, may persevere in the profession of thy name, unto the end; through Jesus Christ, thy dear Son, our Lord. *Amen.*

Then shall he pronounce:
THE BENEDICTION.

XI.

The Order for the Laying of the Corner-Stone of a Church.

The Ministers and the Church-Council shall go up, in procession, to the place where the Church is to be erected, saying the following Psalm:

Psalm cxxii.

I WAS glad when they said unto me, Let us go into the house of the Lord.

2. Our feet shall stand within thy gates, O Jerusalem.

3. Jerusalem is builded as a city that is compact together:

4. Whither the tribes go up, the tribes of the Lord, unto the testimony of Israel, to give thanks unto the name of the Lord.

5. For there are set thrones of judgment, the thrones of the house of David.

6. Pray for the peace of Jerusalem: they shall prosper that love thee.

7. Peace be within thy walls, and prosperity within thy palaces.

8. For my brethren and companions' sakes, I will now say, Peace be within thee.

9. Because of the house of the Lord our God I will seek thy good.

The officiating Minister, standing near the Corner-stone, shall then say:

BELOVED in the Lord,—It is decent, and proper, and in accordance with the Holy Scriptures, that in all our doings we should look up to Almighty God, the Father of lights, from whom cometh down every good gift, and every perfect gift, and beseech him to direct us by his good Spirit, and to prosper the work of our hands with his most gracious help. Especially, therefore, when we are now assembled to commence a house which is to be set apart to his honor and service, and in which his holy name is to be worshipped, his word to be proclaimed, and his sacraments administered, by the ministry whom he hath commissioned, let us humbly and devoutly supplicate his assistance, protection, and blessing.

ALMIGHTY and everlasting God, who art always more ready to hear than we to pray, and art wont to give more than either we desire or deserve; pour down upon us the abundance of thy mercy, forgiving us those things whereof our conscience is afraid, and giving us those good things which we are not worthy to ask, but through the merits and mediation of Jesus Christ thy Son our Lord. *Amen.*

DIRECT us, O Lord, in all our doings, with thy most gracious favor, and further us with thy continual help; that in all our works begun, continued and ended in thee, we may glorify thy holy name; and finally, by thy mercy, obtain everlasting life, through Jesus Christ our Lord. *Amen.*

Then shall the Ministers and all the people say:

OUR Father, who art in heaven; Hallowed be thy name; Thy kingdom come; Thy will be done on earth, as it is in heaven; Give us this day our daily bread; And forgive us our trespasses, as we forgive those who trespass against us; And lead us not into temptation; But deliver us from evil; For thine is the kingdom, and the power, and the glory, for ever and ever. Amen.

Then shall the builders lay the stone in order; the officiating Minister may read the inscription, and mention the articles to be placed in it, and deposit them in the stone. When the stone is set in order and closed, the Minister shall say:

Our help is in the name of the Lord;

The people shall answer:

Who made heaven and earth.

The Minister:

Except the Lord build the house, they labor in vain that build it.

Then the Minister striking the stone three times with a hammer, shall say:

IN the name of the Father, and of the Son, and of the Holy Ghost. Amen.

I lay the Corner-stone of an edifice to be here erected, by the name of ——— Evangelical Lutheran Church, and to be devoted to the service of Almighty God, agreeably to the principles of the Evangelical Lutheran Church in its doctrines, ministry, liturgy, rites and usages.

Other foundation can no man lay than that is laid, which is Jesus Christ—who is God over all, blessed for ever;—in whom we have redemption through his blood, even the forgiveness of sins, according to the riches of his grace. *Amen.*

The Minister shall say:

O Lord, open thou our lips.

The people shall answer:

And our mouth shall show forth thy praise.

Then shall the Minister and all the people say:

I BELIEVE in God the Father Almighty, Maker of heaven and earth.

And in Jesus Christ his only Son, our Lord; Who was conceived by the Holy Ghost, Born of the Virgin Mary; Suffered under Pontius Pilate, Was crucified, dead, and buried; He descended into hell; The third day he rose again from the dead; He ascended into heaven, And sitteth on the right hand of God the Father Almighty; From thence he shall come to judge the quick and the dead.

LAYING OF THE CORNER-STONE. 211

I believe in the Holy Ghost; The holy Christian Church, the Communion of Saints; The forgiveness of sins; The Resurrection of the body; And the life everlasting. Amen.

Minister:

Glory be to the Father, and to the Son, and to the Holy Ghost;

Congregation:

As it was in the beginning, is now, and ever shall be, world without end.

Minister:

Praise ye the Lord.

Congregation:

Let every thing that hath breath praise the Lord. Hallelujah.

Then shall be sung a Hymn of praise, after which the Minister shall say:

Let us pray.

BLESSED be thy name, O Lord, that it hath pleased thee to put it into the hearts of thy servants to commence the erection of a building in which thy holy name is to be worshipped, and the messages of reconciliation are to be proclaimed, and the means of thy grace and our salvation to be administered. Prosper thou them, O God, in this their undertaking; O prosper thou their handywork. Give to the members of this Congregation, unity of council, purity of intention, and a supreme aim at the advancement of thy glory, in promoting the extension and interests of thy holy Church, appointed for the salvation of mankind. Guard by thy providence every thing which may appertain to the building which is now begun in thy fear, and in dependence on thy blessing. Excite the skill and animate the industry of the superintendents and workmen. Protect them from accident, and from danger.

And grant that all who are in any way connected with this temple to be made with hands, may seek those influences of thy Holy Spirit by which their souls will be made temples holy unto thee, and prepared for that city of the living God, which is eternal in the heavens. Animate us all who are here present, O God of our salvation, with the same holy purpose; that, seeking supremely thy mercy and favor, through thy Son our Lord and Saviour Jesus Christ, in the ordinances of thy sanctuary on earth, we may finally be admitted into the company of the redeemed, in the courts of the heavenly Zion. And hasten, we beseech thee, the time when thy Church, at unity in itself, shall serve thee in godly quietness, and when all who profess thy holy name, shall agree in the truth of thy holy word, when all shall be united as true members in the blessed unity of that holy body of which thy Son is the Head; and glorifying thee in thy Church on earth, with one heart and one mouth, be finally numbered with thy saints in thy Church triumphant. All which we ask through the merits of the same thy Son Jesus Christ, who liveth and reigneth with thee and the Holy Spirit, one God, world without end. *Amen.*

Then may follow an
ADDRESS.

After which a Hymn shall be sung, during which a collection may be taken up. Then shall the Minister say:

Let us pray.

O MOST merciful God, gracious Father, we give thee most hearty thanks that thou hast counted us worthy to begin an edifice set apart for thy worship; and we beseech thee so to prosper our work by thy power and goodness, that it may be completed as it is now begun under thy favor and blessing, and that soon a devout and joyful Congregation may be assembled here. O Lord, let thy continual mercy cleanse and defend thy Church. O thou, who art the protector of all that trust in thee, without whom nothing is strong, nothing is holy: increase and multiply upon us thy mercy; that, thou being our ruler and guide, we may so pass through things temporal, that we finally lose not the things eternal. Grant this, O heavenly Father, for Jesus Christ's sake our Lord. *Amen.*

THE BENEDICTION.

XII.

The Order for the Consecration of a Church.

The Ministers and the Church-council going up the aisle of the Church to the Altar, shall repeat the following Introit alternately, the officiating Minister one verse and the others another.

Introit.

HOW amiable are thy tabernacles, O Lord of hosts.

R. My soul longeth, yea fainteth for the courts of the Lord: my heart and my flesh crieth out for the living God. For a day in thy courts is better than a thousand.—Ps. 84.

2. Lift up your heads, O ye gates; even lift them up ye everlasting doors;

R. And the King of glory shall come in.

3. Who is this King of glory?

R. The Lord of hosts, he is the King of glory.—Ps. 24.

When the Ministers have entered within the rails of the Altar, the whole Congregation rising up shall sing or say the

Gloria Patri.

GLORY be to the Father, and to the Son, and to the Holy Ghost;

As it was in the beginning, is now, and ever shall be, world without end. Amen.

Then shall the officiating Minister say:

The Lord be with you.

Answer:

And with thy spirit.

Minister:

Let us pray.

ALMIGHTY and everlasting God, thou art the King of glory; and unto thee alone who dwellest in the high and holy place, be praise and adoration, from the host of heaven, and from all the dwellers upon earth; we thy people come before thy divine presence on this day with joyful hearts, to worship thee in this house which thou hast enabled thy servants to build, and in which thy name shall henceforth be recorded. Receive, we beseech thee, our humble thanksgiving, our cheerful praises, and our sincere adoration, as the first offerings which we here bring before the throne of thy Majesty. Send down thy holy Spirit upon us, that we may lift up holy hands and pure hearts unto thee. Let thy glory fill this house, and thy goodness appear unto thy servants, O Lord our God, who livest and reignest for ever and ever, hear our prayer.— *Amen.*

Then shall the officiating Minister say:

DEARLY beloved in the Lord; for as much as mankind in all ages and in all places have common wants and enjoy common mercies and blessings, it is therefore both reasonable and proper that they should unite with one another in the worship of the Lord of life and the Giver of all good. God our Creator has declared in his holy word, that such worship is acceptable and well-pleasing to him; and his people have at all times experienced, that it is good to say to one another: "O come, let us worship and bow down: let us kneel before the Lord our Maker; for he is our God: and we are the people of his pasture, and the sheep of his fold."

But for the worthy and profitable performance of this sacred duty, it is necessary, not only that special seasons, but also that particular places should be appropriated. Devout and holy men in all ages, have therefore esteemed the erection of houses for the public worship of God a good and profitable work. The erection of them is especially sanctioned by the divine appointment of the tabernacle and temple under the old dispensation; the importance of frequenting them is enforced by the example of our blessed Saviour and the lessons of his apostles; and the consecration of them to the service of the Most High, or the separation of them from worldly and common uses is desirable, that when we meet together for religious purposes, no thought or emotion may be awakened by the place foreign to that great object.

For such a consecration we are now assembled.

Let us hear from the Holy Scriptures, in what manner in ancient time, the first temple of the only true God was dedicated.

Then shall the Minister read

1 KINGS, viii. 22–30. 54–58.

Hear also what the Apostle Paul saith in his Epistle to the

EPHESIANS, ii. 11–22. or
HEBREWS, x. 19–29.

Then shall the Minister and Congregation say:

The Apostles' Creed.

I BELIEVE in God the Father Almighty, Maker of heaven and earth.

And in Jesus Christ his only Son, our Lord; Who was conceived by the Holy Ghost, Born of the Virgin Mary; Suffered under Pontius Pilate, Was crucified, dead, and buried; He descended into hell; The third day he rose again from the dead; He ascended into heaven, And sitteth on the right hand of God the Father Almighty; From thence he shall come to judge the quick and the dead.

I believe in the Holy Ghost; The holy Christian Church, the Communion of Saints; The forgiveness of sins; The resurrection of the body; And the life everlasting. Amen.

Then shall the officiating Minister say:

AND now in this faith, and by the authority committed unto us by the Church of Christ, and with up-lifted hearts to Almighty God, from whom cometh down every blessing; We Ministers of the Church of Christ here assembled, do set apart and consecrate this edifice to a HOUSE OF GOD, to a place of assembly for the Christian Church, under the name of N. N. Evangelical Lutheran Church, separating it henceforth from all unhallowed, ordinary and common uses. We do consecrate it with its pulpit, its altar, its baptismal font and all its parts to the honor of Almighty God our heavenly Father; for the offering up to him of praise and thanksgiving, of prayer and intercession. We consecrate it to the preservation and furtherance of the gospel of his only-begotten Son, our Lord Jesus Christ, the enlightener and Redeemer of the world, that in it the word of the cross may be preached according to the Confessions of our Evangelical Lutheran Church, his holy Sacraments rightly administered to God's believing people, and his religion handed down to the latest generations. We consecrate it to the gracious work of the Holy Ghost, that in it, through his influence the hearts of men may be enlightened, sanctified and sealed unto salvation, and christian unity, love and happiness may be promoted. And to these holy purposes we set apart and consecrate this house, IN THE NAME OF THE FATHER, AND OF THE SON, AND OF THE HOLY GHOST. AMEN.

Ministers and Congregation shall say:

Amen.

BUT, in as much as the consecration of the temple erected by human hands is vain and ineffectual, if not followed by another consecration, even the consecration of those who intend to worship therein, I call upon all of you, who are here present, now to consecrate yourselves anew with all you are and have to the service of our God. To him let our souls be consecrated with all their powers and affections, that they may be renewed after the image of him who hath created them in righteousness and true holiness! To him let our bodies be consecrated, that they may be the temples of the Holy Ghost, and all their members and senses be vessels and instruments sanctified unto God! To him let our calling and station in life be consecrated, that we may faithfully employ them in doing good and glorifying our Father which is in heaven! To him let our whole life be consecrated, that every day may bear witness, that we have not received his grace in vain, but that we are living to his glory.

Thus may the consecration of this house, be accompanied by the consecration of ourselves. And let all the people say : Amen.

Congregation:

Amen.

And now I beseech you, my Christian brethren, to accompany me with your prayers to the God of all grace, that he may grant his blessing to this good work.

Let us pray.

THOU art worthy, O Lord, to receive glory and honor, for thou hast created all things, and by thee they are constantly supported and upheld. Great and marvellous are thy works, Lord God Almighty! just and true are thy ways thou King of Saints. Who shall not fear thee, and glorify thy name? for thou only art holy; thou only art the Lord. All nations shall come and worship before thee, when the counsel of thy love hath been made known unto them.

The heavens, yea, the heaven of heavens cannot contain thee: yet adored be thy name that thou art inviting us to communion with thyself, the everlasting fountain of light, love and joy. Adored be thy name, that it is life eternal to know thee, the only true God, and Jesus Christ whom thou hast sent. Adored be thy name, that thy service is perfect freedom, and that in keeping thy commandments there is great reward.

Receive our thanks, O Father of mercies, for disposing thy servants to erect this house for thine honor, and the edification of immortal souls. Be pleased to accept the consecration of it to thy service, to the religion of Jesus Christ thy Son, and to the operation of the Holy Spirit. Look down in mercy upon this sanctuary, to protect it from every danger; and upon all who shall assemble here from time to time, to gladden them with thy blissful presence. Accomplish in their behalf, O Lord thy promise to dwell in the midst of them, that thou mayest be their God, and that they may be thy people. May they always enter thy sanctuary with reverence, and never leave it without a blessing. And whatsoever they may here do in word or deed, may they do it in the name of the Lord Jesus.

Grant, O Lord, that all who shall be dedicated to thee in this house by the holy Sacrament of Baptism, and thus be received into the covenant of thy grace, may continue to be his true disciples; and that all who shall here renew and confirm the vows made at their Baptism, may be enabled by thy Holy Spirit faithfully to fulfill the same, and to grow in grace unto the end of their lives.

Grant, O Lord, that all who shall at this Altar celebrate the atoning death of their Mediator, by receiving the blessed Sacrament of his body and blood, may be established in their faith, obtain remission of their sins and all other benefits of his passion.

Grant, O Lord, that thy word may at all times be preached here in its purity and power; that it may be received into honest and good hearts, and under the mighty influence of thy Holy Spirit bring forth abundantly the fruits of righteousness and godliness.

Grant, O Lord, that all who shall within these walls show forth thy praise, give thee thanks for thy mercies, confess to thee their sins, seek comfort of thee in all their sorrows and distresses, and implore thy blessing upon themselves and their fellow men, may worship thee in spirit and in truth; that they may receive from thee forgiveness and thy blessing, that putting their whole trust in thee, they may go hence persuaded, that this is indeed a house of God and a gate of heaven.

"Save now, O Lord, we beseech thee; send now prosperity. Let thy work appear unto thy servants, thy glory unto their children; and let the beauty of the Lord our God be upon us." And, "being built upon the foundation of the prophets and apostles, Jesus Christ himself the chief corner-stone, may we grow unto a holy temple in the Lord;" and finally by thy grace, be received into that temple not made with hands in which everlasting songs of praises ascend to thee. *Amen.*

Then shall the Minister and Congregation say:

The Lord's Prayer.

OUR Father, who art in heaven; Hallowed be thy name; Thy kingdom come; Thy will be done on earth, as it is in heaven; Give us this day our daily bread; And forgive us our trespasses, as we forgive those who trespass against us; And lead us not into temptation; But deliver us from evil; For thine is the kingdom, and the power, and the glory, for ever and ever. Amen.

Then shall a Hymn be sung, after which the services shall be continued as in the Order of Morning Service.

www.ingramcontent.com/pod-product-compliance
Lightning Source LLC
Chambersburg PA
CBHW022017220426
43663CB00007B/1118